STORIES
for the
CHILDREN'S
HOUR

Other Books by Kenneth N. Taylor

The Bible in Pictures for Little Eyes
Big Thoughts for Little People
Devotions for the Children's Hour
Giant Steps for Little People
Is Christianity Credible?
The Living Bible
A Living Letter for the Children's Hour
Living Thoughts for the Children's Hour
Wise Words for Little People

STORIES
for the
CHILDREN'S
HOUR

by

Kenneth N. Taylor

MOODY PRESS
CHICAGO

Trade Paperback Edition, 1987

Unless otherwise indicated, Scripture quotations are taken from *The Living Bible* paraphrase.

Moody Press, a ministry of the Moody Bible Institute, is designed for education, evangelization, and edification. If we may assist you in knowing more about Christ and the Christian life, please write us without obligation: Moody Press, c/o MLM, Chicago, Illinois 60610.

Library of Congress Cataloging in Publication Data

Taylor, Kenneth Nathaniel.
    Stories for the children's hour / by Kenneth N. Taylor. — Rev.
ed.
      p.   cm.
    Summary: Forty-eight short stories about everyday occurrences, each of which exemplifies the theme of a Bible passage. Includes study questions and a hymn with each story.
    ISBN 0-8024-2227-6
    1. Children's stories, American.   [1. Christian life—Fiction.
2. Short stories.]   I. Title.
PZ7.T2148St   1987
[Fic]—dc19

                                      87-17367
                                        CIP
                                        AC

5 6 7 Printing/LC/Year 92

Printed in the United States of America

Contents

A Word to Parents

Reading and praying together as a family seems to be becoming a lost art, but I am praying for its return. Six hours (daily average) of watching murders, unfaithfulness, violence, and godlessness on television is the preferred activity in many homes. But that is not God's plan.

I ask all Christian parents (and children) to give God a better chance than He is usually given: take a few minutes at the supper table or at bedtime for reading the Bible or a Bible story book along with a book that applies Bible truths to a child's daily living —like the one you hold in your hand. Let this time together be not only a reading time but a family discussion and life-learning time. The children can tell about incidents at school or play, and parents can tell of their day's activities and thoughts.

As the American family goes down the tube because of the tube, let there be a candle in your home that can do a little—and perhaps a lot—in stabilizing your family for God.

1

The Timmy Club

Timmy was sick, but he was not quite as sick as he had been last month. Then he had been very, very sick indeed. When his father had called the doctor in the middle of the night, the doctor had come and said that Timmy probably had rheumatic fever. Timmy was too sick to care, but his father and mother were very worried. Timmy had to go away to a hospital. When he finally came home again he had to stay in bed for a long time.

Timmy got tired of just lying in bed trying to think of things to do. He wished he would hurry up and get well and strong again, but wishing didn't seem to help. He just had to stay and wait. Timmy thought quite a lot about God while he was sick; he wondered why God had let him be sick. But Timmy loved the Lord Jesus very much and knew that God always knows best and that God would take care of him in whatever way was best. But it was hard just to keep on lying there quietly.

Timmy had many friends in his school, and one day some of them were talking about Timmy. They were sorry that he was sick, sorry that he had to lie there in bed. While they were talking about it, Mary Ann had a very wonderful idea. She said, "Let's start a club. Only it will be a very special kind of club. Let's call it the 'Timmy Club.' This club will do something special for Timmy every day till he gets well."

All the other children were excited about this idea, and they elected Mary Ann to be president of the club.

"Well, first," said the president, "I think we should think of kind things to do for Timmy."

All the children had different ideas, and all the ideas were good. Some of them thought about taking him special things to eat, such as cookies. Some of them thought about games that they could take to him. Some of them thought of taking books from the library to him. Mary Ann wrote down all the ideas. Then she got a pencil and paper and made a list of all the days left in the month, beginning with that very day.

"Today," she said, "someone should bake some cookies to take to Timmy. Who would like to make the cookies?"

"I would," Joe said. "I like to make cookies. I have never made cookies all by myself, but I have helped Mother. I think I can make the cookies."

"All right," said Mary Ann, "but before you take them to Timmy, you must bring one to me so that I can taste it and see if they are good enough."

"Yes," said all the children, "we will all help taste them to be sure that they are good enough."

"Oh, no!" said Mary Ann. "Then all the cookies would be gone and there wouldn't be any left for Timmy. I think it will be enough if I taste them because I am the president."

The other children looked a little bit disappointed, but they did want some cookies to be left for Timmy, so they agreed.

"And tomorrow," said Mary Ann, "because it is Sunday, all of us will go and visit Timmy in the afternoon and tell him what we learned in Sunday school."

"And on Monday, Janet should take him two very interesting and exciting books from the library."

Joe ran home to make the cookies. When he finally had them made (well, his mother helped him a little bit!), he took one of them and ran over to Mary Ann's house to see if she liked it.

"Ummm," said Mary Ann, "this is very good. Maybe I should taste one more just to see if they are all as good."

"Oh, no," said Joe, "there wouldn't be enough for Timmy. And besides," he explained, "all six that I ate were very good."

Timmy thought that the cookies Joe had made were the very best he had ever eaten. "When I get well," he said, "I want you to show me how to make cookies like this."

"OK," said Joe, "I will."

And that night as Timmy was going to sleep he said, "Thank You, Lord, for so many kind friends. Thank You for Joe and the cookies. Thank You for Mary Ann."

So that is how the Timmy Club got started, and it kept going until Timmy got better. Wasn't that a good idea?

Questions:

1. What was the "Timmy Club"?
2. Can you think of some other things the children could have done to make Timmy happy?
3. Do you know any sick child to whom you could be kind by writing a little letter?

A Scripture verse:

Be kind to each other *(Ephesians 4:32)*.

A hymn to sing:

> What a Friend we have in Jesus,
> All our sins and griefs to bear!
> What a privilege to carry
> Everything to God in prayer!

2

Why José Had to Move

Several years ago José and his brother and sister lived with their mother and father in another country. Their country was not like ours. Here we may worship God and tell other people about Jesus. But in the country where José lived, the people became very angry when anyone told them about Jesus. Sometimes they turned away and would not listen. Sometimes they spit at the person who was talking to them about Jesus. Sometimes they tried to hurt the Christians.

José's father and mother and his brother and sister wished that people wouldn't act like that. But they remembered the words of the Lord Jesus when He said, "Blessed are those who are persecuted for righteousness' sake." This means, José's father explained, that God will be especially good to those who are hurt because they love Jesus. They didn't like to be hurt, but they very much liked to please God, and that was far more important.

One night when José's father came home from work, he looked especially sad. After supper he gathered the family around him, and they read from the Bible and prayed. Then José's father told them why he was so sad. That day some men had told him that he could no longer work at his job, because he loved Jesus.

They told him that if he would forget about Jesus, not talk anymore about Him, and not love Him anymore, he could keep his job, and then his family would have enough to eat.

José's father said to his family, "How can we give up Jesus? He died for us, and now we must be willing to die for Him if it's necessary. It is better to die for Jesus and go to heaven than to live without Jesus and then be forever with Satan in hell."

Then José's little brother said something that made them all smile and feel happier.

"Why are you so sad then, Papa?" he asked. "If we are going to see Jesus and go to heaven right away, then why should we be sad?"

"That's right," said José's father. "We will trust the Lord and be happy."

That night about midnight, all of the family were awakened suddenly by a loud noise near their front door. Men were shouting. José's father went to open the door to see what they wanted. "Get out of this house!" they yelled. "Move out of our town at once. We will not have you living here, because you don't belong to our church."

Then Father said, "We will go at once. Come, children. Come, wife." They ran out of the back door just in time, because the men had decided to burn down their house and had already set it on fire.

José and his father and mother and brother and sister walked and walked. They walked all night until they were very tired and hungry. Finally they went to sleep under a big tree. Then they walked and walked and walked some more. They walked until they came to another village where José's uncle lived. José's uncle was surprised to see them. He said that they could stay with him. "You were lucky," he said. "You might all have been killed."

"No," said José, "we were not lucky. It was just that God took care of us and decided to let us live longer to serve Him."

"Yes," said José's uncle, "you are right."

Questions:

1. Was José's family lucky?
2. Could God have kept the men away from José's house?
3. Does God always keep us from getting hurt? Why not?
4. Does God always love us?

A Scripture verse:

Others were laughed at and their backs cut open with whips, and some were chained in dungeons *(Hebrews 11:36)*.

A hymn to sing:

> God will take care of you,
> Through every day,
> O'er all the way;
> He will take care of you,
> God will take care of you.

3

Mr. Bert the Cat

The children next door were moving away.

Gretchen and Robert were sad as they watched the moving truck back up to the house where their little friend Linda lived. Linda wouldn't be able to play with them anymore.

Yesterday afternoon they had had a tea party with Linda, because Linda was going away. Mother had even made special cookies for them.

Then, last night Linda and her mother and daddy got into the car and waved good-bye.

Mr. Bert was the name of Linda'a cat. Linda loved her cat very much, but her mother said it would be better to give Mr. Bert to someone in the neighborhood and get another cat for their new home. Her mother told her that she would get her a little kitten as soon as they moved.

Linda was very sorry that she couldn't have Mr. Bert, but she was glad that Mother said she might have another cat at her new home.

So Mr. Bert was given to a neighbor down the street who wanted a cat and was fond of Mr. Bert.

That night the children prayed that Linda might be happy in her new home, and they also prayed that Mr. Bert might like his new home.

As the children were going to sleep they thought they heard Mr. Bert meowing. They thought that perhaps he had come back to try to find Linda, and they felt very sorry for him.

The next day they thought they heard Mr. Bert meowing again, but after they had looked all around the yard and couldn't find him, they decided that they had just thought they had heard him.

But that night they heard the meowing again, and they were just sure it was Mr. Bert.

Gretchen and Robert asked Mother if they could go out in the yard with a flashlight and try to find the cat, and Mother said they might.

They looked behind all the bushes, and behind the garage, and in the garage, but they couldn't find Mr. Bert. They didn't hear any more meowing, so they went back into the house.

A whole week went by, and they kept thinking that they could hear Mr. Bert, but they could never find him. Even Mother thought that she could hear him sometimes.

One afternoon the children were playing in Linda's yard, and they looked in the windows of the empty house. What do you think they saw?

It was Mr. Bert lying on the floor. At first they thought that he was asleep. They rattled on the window to wake him up and called to him, but Mr. Bert just barely moved and opened his eyes a little bit. Then the children knew that he was very sick.

"He must be almost dead," Robert said, "because he hasn't had any food or water for a whole week!"

The children rushed over to call Mother, and she came to see.

"How did Mr. Bert ever get in there?" Mother wondered. Then she said, "He must have slipped in when the movers were taking out the furniture, and no one noticed him. Poor Mr. Bert, how will we ever get him out?"

Mother went into the house and telephoned the neighbors to see if any of them had a key, but none of them did.

The children thought and thought about what to do.

That afternoon George, a new boy in the neighborhood, came over to play with Gretchen and Robert. When they showed him Mr. Bert, he said, "Aw, it's just a cat. Let him die."

Gretchen and Robert didn't like him to say that.

"It's not just a cat," said Gretchen. "It's Mr. Bert, and we're going to get him out."

"How are you going to get him out?" asked George. "You can't do it without breaking a window or something, and then you would have to pay for it."

"That's a good idea!" said Robert excitedly. "We'll get him out by breaking the window."

"It will probably cost you five dollars for a new window," said George, "and no old cat's worth five dollars. You could buy loads of ice cream cones for that."

Robert thought about the money he had in his piggy bank, and how long it had taken him to save it, and about the nice things he intended to buy.

Then Robert made up his mind. "Gretchen," he said, "would you get a yardstick to measure the window while I get a brick?"

Soon Gretchen was back with the ruler, and Robert was there with the brick. Gretchen brought a blanket, too, and held it against the window so that when Robert broke the window he wouldn't be hurt with flying glass.

Very carefully Robert felt where the window was and began to hit it a little bit with the brick. He kept hitting it a little bit harder and a little bit harder until the window cracked. Pretty soon pieces of the glass fell out. Robert took away the blanket and began to take out the other pieces of sharp glass left in the window.

Mr. Bert was too sick to crawl over to him, so Robert had to crawl through the window, then go and pick him up. He handed him out the window to Gretchen, who quickly took him to her mother to feed and take care of.

Then Robert took his money and, after measuring the window to get the size of glass, went down to the hardware store and bought a new pane of glass to put into the broken window frame.

When Gretchen's and Robert's father came home that evening, he helped them put in the new glass.

That night Gretchen said to Robert, "I'm sorry that it cost five dollars to rescue Mr. Bert, but I am so glad you did it."

"So am I," said Robert. "I think it is what Jesus wanted me to do. Someday He will probably give me the five dollars back and much more besides!"

Questions:

1. Does Jesus want us to be kind to animals?
2. Do you think it was worth more than four ice cream cones to rescue Mr. Bert?
3. Did Robert use his money wisely?

A Scripture verse:

Happy are the kind and merciful, for they shall be shown mercy *(Matthew 5:7)*.

A hymn to sing:

> Take my life, and let it be
> Consecrated, Lord, to Thee;
> Take my hands, and let them move
> At the impulse of Thy love,
> At the impulse of Thy love.

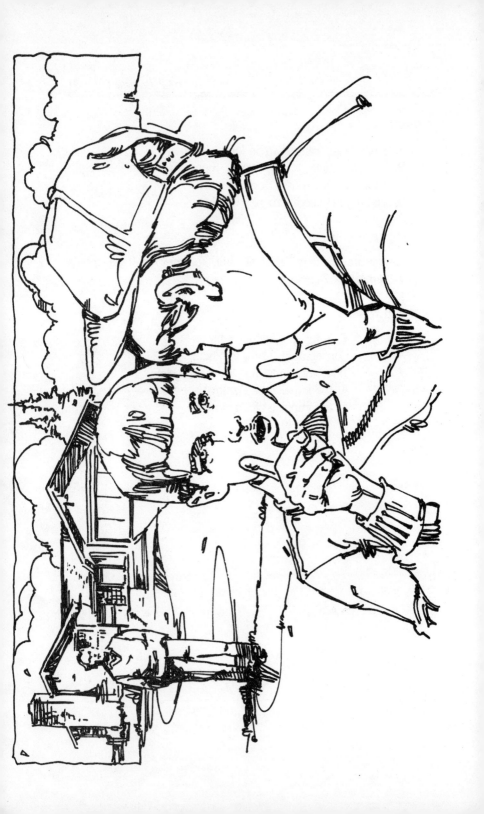

4

The New Neighbors

The Jones family, who moved in next to Terry and Mark, had five children. The oldest was eleven years old, and the littlest one was just a few weeks old.

"Oh, boy!" said Terry to Mark, "if we can get them to come to Sunday school with us, we sure can get a lot of points in the contest for bringing new kids!"

"Yes," said Mark, "but there is something a lot more important than getting points. If those kids don't know the Lord Jesus, maybe we can tell them about Him, and get them to Sunday school so that they can learn about Him."

After a few days, when all the children had become good friends, Terry and Mark asked them if they would go along to Sunday school—and do you know what they found out?

The Jones family had never been to Sunday school, not once in their whole lives! Not any of them!

Terry and Mark were so surprised that they almost had to sit down to catch their breath.

Never been to Sunday school? They had never heard of such a thing.

Terry and Mark had been to Sunday school almost every week since they were two years old, and they wouldn't miss it for anything.

No one in the place where they used to live had ever asked the Jones children to go to Sunday school, so they ran in to ask their father if they could go.

"No," said Mr. Jones, "I don't think so. Sunday school doesn't help anybody, and besides there are things we can do around here on Sunday mornings."

The Jones children and Terry and Mark were disappointed. Terry and Mark were surprised that Mr. Jones thought Sunday school didn't do anyone any good.

"I think it has helped us," Terry said.

"I know it has," said Mark, "because now we know about the Lord Jesus, and He helps us to be good and to talk to other people about God."

"Well," said Mr. Jones, "we'll see about that. If going to Sunday school has helped you as much as you think it has, then I'll be able to find out about it by watching the way you act."

When Terry and Mark were eating supper that evening, they told their mother and father what Mr. Jones had said.

"Well," said Father, "that's a real challenge. If you boys act like Christians, Mr. Jones will be able to see a difference between you and children who aren't Christians. And if he sees a real difference, he will let his children go to Sunday school. So it's up to you, it seems."

"It's up to all of us," said Mother, "because if Mr. Jones sees that all of us as a family are different because of the Lord Jesus living in our home, then he will want the Lord Jesus to live in his home too."

That night they all prayed that they might be kind and courteous and obedient and helpful to one another and to the other people in the neighborhood, so that Mr. Jones could tell that it makes a difference to belong to Jesus.

After that, whenever Terry and Mark began to quarrel, one or the other of them was sure to say, "Shh! Remember about Mr. Jones. He might be listening."

And then the other one would think of something else and would say, "Yes, and Jesus is listening and watching us," and they would stop quarreling.

Whenever Mother wanted them to do something and they wanted to do something else, they thought about Jesus watching them. So instead of being grouchy about their work they were happy and pleasant.

And you know, it worked!

A few weeks later when Terry and Mark were at the neighbors' playing, Mr. Jones came out in the yard where they were.

"What day is tomorrow, boys?" he asked.

"Sunday," said Terry.

"Are you going to Sunday school in the morning?" asked Mr. Jones.

"Sure," said Mark, "just like we always do."

Then Mr. Jones said something that surprised all the children very much.

He said, "How would you like to invite my children to go along with you? If your father is willing to lead the way in his car, I'll follow in my van and we'll all get there at the same time. Then you can show my children where to go."

"Oh, that would be wonderful!" said Terry and Mark at the same time.

Then they ran home to ask their father about it.

Father went right over to see Mr. Jones. "Why don't you and Mrs. Jones come along with us for the mothers and fathers' class too?" he asked Mr. Jones.

"Well," said Mr. Jones, "perhaps we will. You know, I've been watching you folks for the last few weeks, and there is something different. I think it's because you go to Sunday school."

"Well," said Father, "that isn't exactly it, although that's part of it. The real reason is that the Lord Jesus lives at our house."

Then Father talked to Mr. Jones for a long time about how the Lord Jesus was sent by God to die to take away our sins. "All we have to do," Father explained, "is to ask Jesus to save us."

The next morning the whole Jones family went to Sunday school for the first time in their lives. It wasn't very long after that that Mr. Jones came over one evening to tell Father that both he and Mrs. Jones had asked the Lord Jesus to come into their home.

Terry and Mark were in the other room and heard their father and mother and Mr. and Mrs. Jones talking together.

"It sure pays to live for Jesus, doesn't it?" said Terry.

And Mark replied, "It sure does."

Questions:

1. How did Mr. Jones decide whether or not to let his children go to Sunday school?
2. Does Sunday school help you? How?
3. What did Terry and Mark's father say was the real reason for their being good neighbors?

Some Scripture verses:

Don't hide your light! Let it shine for all; let your good deeds glow for all men to see, so that they will praise your heavenly Father *(Matthew 5:15-16)*.

A song to sing:

> This little light of mine,
> Yes! I'm gonna let it shine,
> This little light of mine,
> Yes, I'm gonna let it shine,
> Let it shine, let it shine, let it shine.

5

The June Bride

It was springtime. The birds were singing, the grass was green, and everyone at Susan's house should have been very happy. Susan's pretty aunt was going to be married the next week to a nice man named John. Susan liked John. Whenever he came over to see Aunt Jane, he and little Susan had a talk.

Aunt Jane was very happy, but Susan's mother seemed sad. Sometimes Susan heard her mother and Aunt Jane talking in the next room. Mother kept saying, "But, Jane, he isn't a Christian, and you shouldn't marry him." Susan knew that they were talking about John. Susan knew that John wasn't a Christian because she had asked him once. He had just laughed and said, "No, but I guess I'm about as good as most Christians."

So when Susan's mother would say that John wasn't a Christian, Jane would say, "Well, he will be; I'm sure I can get him to love the Lord as I do."

"Jane, it just doesn't work that way," Susan's mother would say. "What if he doesn't become a Christian? Then what are you going to do? How can you keep loving the Lord Jesus the way you want to when you are married to someone who laughs at you all the time?"

"But I love John very much," said Jane, "so I think it will be all right."

"Love isn't enough," Susan's mother would say. "Obeying God is more important. He has told you not to marry a person who isn't a Christian."

Aunt Jane and John were married the next week and went away on a trip. When they came back they lived in another city not far from the town where Susan lived.

Aunt Jane invited Susan to come and stay for a few days, so Daddy drove her there in the car and left her for a whole week.

Susan had a nice time, but she was sad because it didn't seem like Aunt Jane loved the Lord Jesus quite as much as she used to do. When Susan waited to have prayer said before they ate their meals, Aunt Jane seemed embarrassed, and Uncle John said, "Go right ahead, Susan. We don't wait for prayer here." Susan didn't like to eat without thanking God for the food, so she said the prayer in her heart, even though no one heard her except God.

When supper was over at home, Daddy and Mother and the children would all sing and pray and read the Bible. But no one ever talked about God at Aunt Jane and Uncle John's house.

One day Susan asked Aunt Jane about it, and Aunt Jane told her that Uncle John didn't like God. "We shouldn't have been married," she told Susan. "Your mother was right, but now it's too late." And Aunt Jane began to cry.

Susan couldn't do anything about it, but she does pray every day that Uncle John will see how much he needs the Lord Jesus.

Questions:

1. Why was Susan's mother sad?
2. Why did Aunt Jane think it would be all right to marry John?
3. Was Aunt Jane right?

A Scripture verse:

Don't be chained to those who do not love the Lord *(2 Corinthians 6:14).*

A hymn to sing:

> Trust and obey,
> For there's no other way
> To be happy in Jesus,
> But to trust and obey.

6

Carol's Bible

Carol Todd was so excited that she just couldn't stand still. Whenever she thought about her gift she couldn't keep from jumping up and down and clapping her hands. Carol was going to have a Bible all her own! The next Sunday the superintendent was giving Bibles to all the children in her class who were being promoted to the junior department.

Just think! Her very own Bible! And she could even read it. She knew she could because she had read a little bit from Father's big Bible. And if she could read Father's Bible then she could read the Bible that would soon be hers.

There was only one thing she still had to do and that was to learn the Twenty-third Psalm. She asked Mother to help her, and she said it over and over and over again until she had every word just right. Then she ran over to the home of Miss Jones, her teacher, and said it to her. Miss Jones said that she could have her Bible the next Sunday.

On the next Sunday morning from the first moment she woke up, Carol knew something very special was going to happen. At first she couldn't think what it was, and then all of a sudden it jumped into her mind. Today was the day she was going to get her very own Bible.

When it came time for Carol's class to get their promotion certificates and their Bibles, Carol stood up in front of the whole Sunday school—and all the big people too—and recited the Twenty-third Psalm. Miss Jones had asked her to do it so that everyone would know that all the children in the class knew the psalm. Carol made one little mistake but the superintendent didn't seem to notice it.

When she had finished, the superintendent gave Carol her Bible. She clasped it to her heart and said, "Thank you," very loudly.

The superintendent smiled and said, "You're welcome." Then he said, "Carol, what are you going to do with that Bible?"

"Oh," said Carol, "I am going to take it home and read it."

"Good," said the superintendent. "I want you to read from it every day. I want you to start with the book of John in the New Testament and read one chapter this afternoon. Then read another chapter tomorrow, and one each day following. You must read the Bible and learn for yourself what God wants of you, now that you are a big girl and can read. You can read your Bible and study it carefully and do what it says. Then you will be a real Bible girl, and the Lord will know you are one of His very best helpers."

After dinner was over and the dishes had been washed, Carol took out her new Bible and opened it carefully and found the book of John. Then she started reading the first chapter. She didn't understand all of it, but she found several things that she could understand, and she thought about them. Then Carol bowed her head and prayed. She said, "Thank You, God, for giving me this Bible. Thank You for telling us so many things in it. Help me to be a Bible girl all the rest of my life."

Questions:

1. Why did Carol want the Bible?
2. What did the superintendent mean when he told Carol he wanted her to be a Bible girl?
3. Do we need to do what the Bible tells us or just read it?

A Scripture verse:

Your words are a flashlight to light the path ahead of me, and keep me from stumbling *(Psalm 119:105)*.

A hymn to sing:

> Sing them over again to me,
> Wonderful words of Life;
> Let me more of their beauty see,
> Wonderful words of Life.

7

The Art Contest

"**M**other," said Ann, rushing in from school, "there's going to be an art contest at school tomorrow, and I'm going to win it."

"That's fine," said Mother. "How do you know you'll win?"

"Because I have a good idea," Ann told her mother. "It's such a good idea I know I'll win."

Ann went up to her room and looked and looked until she found a certain book. One part of the book showed drawings made by seven-year-old children. One of the drawings was especially good and had won a prize. It showed a big red house with a little girl leaning out of the window looking at a bird. Ann planned to copy this picture for the art contest.

Of course, Ann knew that this would be wrong, but she was going to do it anyway. She got out her crayons and tried to draw the picture. She tried it several times and finally did it without looking. Then she knew she could draw it the next day without the book, and everyone would think it was her own picture. That would be like telling a lie, Ann knew, but she tried not to think about it.

The next morning Ann ran happily to school. The contest was to be right after recess, and she could hardly wait.

After recess Miss Price said, "Now, children, we are going to have our contest. You may take out your crayons and begin." Ann remembered how to make the drawing in the book and soon had it finished. She took it proudly to the teacher.

When all the pictures had been handed in and Miss Price had looked at them, she decided that Ann's picture was the best. The other children thought so too, and Ann was very happy. At lunchtime she ran home to tell her mother.

When lunch was ready Ann bowed her head to ask the blessing and started to say, "Father, thank You for this food and because I won the contest this morning." But just as she was beginning to say "Father," she thought of something. All of a sudden she knew that God had been watching her when she was learning to copy the picture in that book, and she knew God wasn't pleased. So she didn't say anything to God about winning the contest but just said, "Thank You for the food. In Jesus' name. Amen." And she didn't feel very hungry after that.

All afternoon when she was reading or doing arithmetic or spelling, she kept thinking, *God is sorry I did it. He is displeased.* She thought about it so much that she began to feel sick. She had done something very wrong. But surely she couldn't stand up and tell the class about it. They would all know how she had cheated.

But finally she could stand it no longer. She knew how sorry Jesus was, and she didn't want Him to be sorry any longer.

She couldn't make herself to go up and tell Miss Price, but she wrote a little note, and this is what it said:

"Dear Miss Price, I am sorry to tell you that the picture I drew was copied, so I didn't win the contest. Ann."

Ann gave the note to Miss Price as she went out with the other children for afternoon recess. She didn't want to play; she didn't want to do anything. Then Miss Price came out and found her and put her arm around her.

"Ann," said Miss Price, "thank you for telling me, but I knew anyway. You see, when I was a little girl there was an art contest, and I won first prize. It was my picture that was used in the book, so I was very surprised when you handed me your drawing this morning. Now let's go in, and I'll help you tell the other children."

Ann was ashamed, but with help from Miss Price she told the other children all about it. And because Ann went to a Christian school, Miss Price said, "And now let's tell God about it too. When we tell Him we are sorry for our sins, He forgives us." So they all bowed their heads, and Miss Price prayed.

That night Ann told her mother, and when she went to bed she knelt down and said to God: "Thank You, God, for sending Jesus to die for me, and thank You for forgiving me for lying about the picture."

And as Ann went off to sleep she said, "Oh, I'm so glad I told Miss Price. Now I can be happy when I wake up. Thank You again, Lord Jesus, for forgiving me."

Questions:

1. Why did Ann think she would win the art contest?
2. How long was she happy about winning it?
3. How do you think Ann felt when she told the other children what she had done?

A Scripture verse:

Don't tell lies to each other *(Colossians 3:9).*

A hymn to sing:

> I will sing of my Redeemer
> And His wondrous love to me;
> On the cruel cross He suffered,
> From the curse to set me free.

8

Billy Sings a Song

Billy Adams sat on his porch, loudly singing the song he had learned at Bible club a few days before. The song went like this:

> I will make you fishers of men,
> Fishers of men,
> Fishers of men;
> I will make you fishers of men,
> If you follow Me.

Billy liked to sing, and that's why he sang the song over and over again.

It was a warm day, so Billy went in to ask his mother if he could have a drink of lemonade. She said, "Billy, what was that song I heard you singing out there on the porch?"

"A song?" asked Billy, surprised. "Was I singing? Oh, yes, I remember now. I was singing, 'I will make you fishers of men.' "

"Did you learn that at Bible club?" his mother asked.

"Yes," said Billy, "I think it is a very nice song. Shall I sing it for you?"

"Please," said Mother.

So Billy sang the song for her twice.

"Well," said Mother, "I think you ought to think about what you are singing and try to understand it too. Then you can sing it even better."

"That's a good idea," Billy said, and he went back on the porch with his glass of lemonade to think about the song. He thought and thought, and the more he thought about it the more he wondered just what it did mean. He knew about fishing for fish, but he had never thought about fishing for people. He finally decided there was a lot of difference in fishing for people and fishing for fish. When you catch a fish, you hurt them, but when you catch people, you help them. He decided that by "fishing" the song meant to tell people about Jesus and bring them to Him.

All of a sudden Billy jumped up off the porch with one big jump. You could always tell when Billy had a big idea because it always made him jump. This big jump meant that he had a very big idea.

Then Billy rushed into the house to tell his mother.

"Mother," he said, "I have the best idea and the biggest idea that I have ever had!"

"Oh!" said his mother. "That must be a very big idea if it is the best and the biggest you have ever had. Tell me what it is."

"Mother," said Billy, "I'm going to be a fisherman. I'm going to fish for people instead of fishing for fish. I'm going to do just like the song says and ask Jesus to make me a good fisherman for Him."

"That's a very good idea," said his mother. "How are you going to start?"

"First," said Billy, "I'm going over to see Doug and see if he will go to Sunday school with me next Sunday." And off Billy ran to find Doug.

Doug was sitting on his porch reading a book. "Hi, Doug!" Billy called. "I'm a fisherman, and I want you to be a fish."

"But I don't want to be a fish," said Doug. "I want to read this book."

"No," said Billy, "you have to be a fish because I've just learned a song. Do you want me to sing it to you?"

"OK," said Doug. And so Billy sang his chorus again.

> I will make you fishers of men,
> Fishers of men,
> Fishers of men;
> I will make you fishers of men,
> If you follow Me.

"What does the song mean?" asked Doug.

"It means that you ought to come to Sunday school next Sunday and learn about Jesus," said Billy.

"I'd like to go to Sunday school with you," said Doug. "Let's go ask my mother."

So the two boys went in to see Doug's mother, and she said that she would like to have Doug go with Billy to Sunday school. Billy said he would stop by for Doug and they would go together.

"Now," said Billy to Doug, "you come over with me to see David, and we'll ask him to come to Sunday school too."

So the two boys went over to see David, and he was mowing his lawn. He was hot and tired and didn't want to mow the lawn. But it had to be done.

"Hi, David!" said Billy and Doug together. "We want you to come to Sunday school with us next Sunday."

David wasn't feeling very agreeable because of the lawn mowing. He didn't want to do what the boys wanted because he felt disagreeable. "No," said Dave, "I don't want to go to Sunday school."

"I know what," said Doug, "if we help you with your lawn this afternoon, will you go to Sunday school with us next Sunday?"

"Oh, yes," said David quickly. "I'd be glad to do that."

So Billy and Doug helped David with the lawn, then said,

"David, would you come with us to ask Carolyn if she could come to Sunday school next Sunday?"

"Sure," said David, and so the three boys went over to Carolyn's house. Carolyn was making some cookies. Of course, her mother was helping her—or maybe she was helping her mother. Anyway, some of the cookies had just been taken out of the oven, and she gave one to each of the boys.

"Yum, yum," they said. "These are very good cookies, Carolyn. We came over to see if you would come to Sunday school with us next Sunday morning." Carolyn's mother said that she might go, and Carolyn said that she would if her neighbor Kathy would go too.

So the three boys and Carolyn went next door to see Kathy. "Kathy, will you come to Sunday school with us next Sunday?" they asked.

"Yes," said Kathy, "I'd like to come."

That night when Billy got home, his mother asked, "Well, Mr. Fisherman, how did you get along?"

And Billy told her that Doug and David and Carolyn and Kathy were all going to Sunday school with him.

Billy's mother was surprised and pleased. "You are a very good fisherman, Billy," she said. "I think Jesus must have helped you. And now we will pray that each of the children will come to love Jesus when they go to Sunday school next Sunday."

When Dad came home they told him about all the new children going to Sunday school. That night before Billy went to bed, the whole family prayed about the next Sunday.

Questions:

1. What does the song mean when it says, "I will make you fishers of men"?
2. Who helps us tell others about Jesus?
3. Can you think of some friends who don't go to Sunday school very often?
4. Are you a good fisherman?

A Scripture verse:

I will make you fishermen for the souls of men *(Mark 1:17).*

A hymn to sing:

> I love to tell the story—
> It will be my theme in glory—
> To tell the old, old story
> Of Jesus and His love.

9

The Book That Wasn't Right

As the children walked home from school they talked about what they had read in their science book and what the teacher had said.

Their science book had said some very strange things. It said that nobody knew how the first person became alive. It said that millions and millions of years ago, somewhere on the edge of some ocean, a little speck of life began. As more millions of years went by that little speck of life grew bigger and bigger, and divided into many different kinds of birds and animals. Finally after millions of years more, some of the animals began to look more and more like men, and finally one became the first human being. Someday, the book had said, it is probable that people will not look like they do now but will be stronger and more beautiful and more intelligent.

The children were quite surprised when they read this in their science book. They knew that this was not what the Bible said.

The teacher could tell that they were surprised, and she said: "Children, you might as well learn now that books are not always right. Don't believe everything you read. Books are often

written by men and women who know a great deal, but they do
not know everything. They do not know how men and women
first came to be. The person who wrote this book has written
down what he guesses. He thinks that is how it happened, but he
does not know."

"Does anyone know how it happened?" Bob wanted to
know.

The teacher smiled. "Does anyone want to answer that
question?" she asked.

Kevin put up his hand. "All right," said the teacher, "you tell
us."

Kevin said, "God made Adam and Eve and put them in the
Garden of Eden. He had made Adam from the dust of the ground
and had made Eve from one of Adam's ribs."

"That is what the Bible says, isn't it, Kevin? Now, children,
there are many people who do not believe the Bible, and so they
do not know how the first man became alive."

"Do you believe the Bible?" the children asked the teacher.

"Well," said the teacher, "I don't know. I'm not sure if I'm a
Christian. Sometimes I think that probably God made Adam and
Eve and put them in the Garden of Eden, just as Kevin said. But I
don't know. Sometimes I think it didn't happen that way."

That night Kevin told his father about what happened at
school. "I thought everybody believed the Bible," Kevin said.

"Oh, no," said Father, "lots of people don't. There are lots of
people who are not Christians and don't have the Lord Jesus as
their Savior."

"If so many people don't think the Bible is true, how can we
know it is?" Kevin asked.

"There are several ways," Father said. "For one thing, because it is a book that tells about many things that were going to
happen, and hundreds of years later did happen. The Bible
wouldn't have known these things were going to happen unless
God wrote it. God made Adam, and He tells us about it in the
Bible.

"Another way we know the Bible is true is that it is not like an ordinary book. It is a miracle Book, and it changes people's lives. People who have been very bad read the Bible and hear about the Lord Jesus, then they become His children and are good. No other book is able to make people change that way, at least not for very long."

Kevin said, "Then the science books aren't always right, and the teachers aren't always right, but the Bible is."

"Yes," said Father, "remember that as long as you live."

Questions:

1. Should we believe everything we read in books?
2. What is the only Book we can believe? Why?
3. Are teachers always right in everything they think?
4. Can you think of one reason we know the Bible is true?

A Scripture verse:

Oh Timothy, don't fail to do those things that God entrusted to you. Keep out of foolish arguments with those who boast of their "knowledge" and thus prove their lack of it *(1 Timothy 6:20)*.

A hymn to sing:

Standing, standing,
Standing on the promises of God my Savior;
Standing, standing,
I'm standing on the promises of God.

10

The Broken Toy

One day when Bruce White was out playing in his yard he noticed some birds sitting on a telephone wire. Bruce was not a very kind boy, and he decided to try to hit the birds with stones. He picked up several stones from the side of the road. The birds were sitting quite close to a window of Mrs. Hamilton's house. He had to be careful not to hit the window with the stones when he was trying to hit the birds.

Bruce didn't hit the birds. He kept trying and trying. The birds didn't seem to think that he could hit them either, because they just kept sitting there.

Finally Bruce forgot all about the window and threw a stone as hard as he could. But the stone didn't hit the birds; instead, it went right through Mrs. Hamilton's window. The glass made a terrible noise as it fell into pieces on the ground. Mrs. Hamilton came running out to see what was the matter.

"Oh, Bruce!" she said, "you have broken my window!"

Bruce felt bad that he had broken the window. He said, "I'm sorry, Mrs. Hamilton. I didn't mean to do it. I was throwing stones at some birds that were sitting on the wire. I'm sorry."

"Well," said Mrs. Hamilton, "it's good that you are sorry about it, but being sorry doesn't fix the window. I guess I will have to telephone Mr. Hamilton and ask him to bring home another piece of glass."

"How much will it cost?" asked Bruce. "I should pay for it."

"Yes," said Mrs. Hamilton, "I suppose you should. It will probably cost about four dollars."

"Four dollars!" exclaimed Bruce. "Oh, my. I don't have four dollars. I only have fifty-seven cents when I last counted."

"Well, then," said Mrs. Hamilton, "you won't need to pay for the window. I will forgive you, and I will pay for it myself."

"Oh, thank you, Mrs. Hamilton! Thank you very much."

When Bruce got home he found his little sister Ruth playing with one of his balloons. Just as Bruce walked into the room where Ruth was playing, the balloon popped.

"You bad, bad girl!" said Bruce. "You've broken my balloon."

Ruth was very sorry. She said, "I am sorry, Bruce. I didn't mean to do it. I was just playing it, and it popped."

"Being sorry doesn't fix the balloon," said Bruce. "You have to pay for it."

"How much will it cost?" asked little Ruth.

"It will cost ten cents," he said. "Give me ten cents right now."

"But I don't have ten cents," said Ruth. "I only have eight cents in my piggy bank."

"Then give me the eight cents," demanded Bruce, "and you will have to pay me the rest later on. You are a bad girl for breaking my balloon."

So Ruth got the eight cents from her piggy bank and gave it to Bruce. "Don't forget, you still owe me two cents," Bruce said angrily, as he grabbed the money and put it into his pocket.

Ruth went outdoors crying. Mrs. Hamilton was in her backyard hanging out clothes. "What is the matter, Ruth?" she asked.

Ruth told Mrs. Hamilton about breaking Bruce's balloon and taking all of the pennies out of her piggy bank to pay him back.

Mrs. Hamilton was now angry with Bruce. She called him and said, "Bruce, I have changed my mind about the four dollars that it will cost to fix that window. I was planning to pay it, but after I forgave you all that money, you would not even forgive little Ruth ten cents. You don't deserve to be forgiven the four dollars, and you must pay it."

Then Bruce was very sorry that he had not forgiven Ruth, as Mrs. Hamilton had forgiven him.

Boys and girls, do you know that God has told us that we must forgive one another because He has forgiven us? He has forgiven us for all the wrong things we have done. He paid the price by giving His life and dying for us. Since He did that, we certainly ought to forgive the little things that people do to us that displease us. So the very next time someone breaks one of your toys and is sorry, you can say, "That's all right; God has forgiven me for things I have done that He doesn't like, and so I gladly forgive you for breaking my toy."

Questions:

1. Why didn't Mrs. Hamilton make Bruce pay for the window at first?
2. Do you think there was something wrong in Bruce's heart when he wouldn't forgive his little sister?
3. Do you think God would like it if, after He has forgiven you, you would not forgive someone else?

A Scripture verse:

And forgive us our sins, just as we have forgiven those who have sinned against us *(Matthew 6:12)*.

A hymn to sing:

Search me, O God, and know my heart today;
Try me, O Savior, know my thoughts, I pray:
See if there be some wicked way in me;
Cleanse me from every sin, and set me free.

11

Marcia Cohen's Discovery

Marcia Cohen lived in a big house down at the end of the street. She was a dear little girl who was always trying to help other people. She and Katherine Blake often used to walk to school together, because they were good friends.

One day after school, Katherine was walking home and she caught up with Marcia. She was surprised to see that Marcia was crying. "Why, Marcia," she said, "what is the matter?"

At first Marcia wouldn't tell Katherine why she was crying. Then Katherine noticed that there were other boys and girls walking along across the street. They were pointing at Marcia and laughing. "You bad children," Katherine called to them. "Why are you teasing Marcia?"

Then the children started singing:

> Marcia's a Jew,
> Marcia's a Jew;
> We don't like her,
> And we hate her, too.

"Come on, Marcia," said Katherine, "let's hurry home. Don't pay attention to those children." The two little girls ran home and tried to forget the bad children by playing with dolls, which they both liked to do.

That night Katherine told her father and mother what had happened. "Were they calling her bad names?" she wanted to know. "What is a Jew?"

Father seemed angry. "Poor little girl!" he said. "Don't you know what a Jew is, Katherine? Don't you remember the Old Testament stories about Abraham and Isaac and Jacob and the people of Israel? The Jews are the Israelites."

Katherine's eyes began dancing with joy. "You mean that Marcia is one of the children of Israel?"

"Yes," said Father, "just as Queen Esther was. Abraham had a child, and his name was Isaac. Isaac had a child, and his name was Jacob. Jacob had twelve sons, and they had children, and their children had children; and so it was for hundreds of years until finally Marcia was born. There are millions of other Jews in various parts of this country and in various parts of the world. All of them come from Abraham."

"But why did they call her names?" asked Katherine.

"Many people don't like Jews," her father explained. "They think Jews are sometimes too bold and sometimes make more money than people who aren't Jews and that some Jews aren't as fair as they should be. Of course, that is also true of people who are not Jews."

"Marcia is very kind. She is always fair," Katherine said. "They shouldn't make fun of her."

"No," said Father, "they certainly should not. The Jews are God's people, and God has said that He would punish people who are unkind to them, but He will bless those who are kind to the Jews."

"Are Jews Christians?" Katherine wanted to know.

"No," explained Father, "usually not. They do not realize that Jesus died for them. But some of them become Christians, and then they are part of God's family in just the same way that we are."

"I wish I could keep the children from calling Marcia names," said Katherine.

"I doubt if you can," said Father, "but at least you can be a friend to Marcia, and you can tell her about Jesus."

"That's a good idea," Katherine said. "I'm going to tell her right now, and then she won't be unhappy about what happened this afternoon."

And off Katherine ran to find Marcia, to tell her the good news.

Questions:

1. Is it kind make fun of other people?
2. Who are the Jews?
3. What has God promised to those who are kind to the Jews?
4. What will happen to people who dislike the Jews?
5. How can we be truly kind in our hearts to people we don't like?

A Scripture verse:

I will bless those who bless you, and curse those who curse you *(Genesis 12:3)*.

A hymn to sing:

> He leadeth me, He leadeth me!
> By His own hand He leadeth me!
> His faithful follower I would be,
> For by His hand He leadeth me.

12

The Broken Kite

Children at Pollybrook School loved the windy weather. Their school was in a field on the side of a hill. The woods were far enough away so that the field made a wonderful place to fly kites. Many boys brought their kites to school and flew them during recess. Mr. Smith, who had the little store at the crossroads, sold the parts to the kites, and the boys and girls put them together.

Jim was proud of his kite. His flew the highest of any in the whole school. Jim had made the kite with his father's help. It was stronger and better than the kites Mr. Smith sold. All the other children liked to watch it flying there in the sky.

David was a friend of Jim's. The boys often played together. One day David stayed after school to help the teacher. After he erased the blackboards, he went into the coat room to put on his jacket to go home, and he saw Jim's kite. The wind was blowing nicely outside, and David thought, "Oh, how much fun it would be to fly Jim's kite! But Jim isn't here, so I can't ask him." Then David thought, "I don't think that Jim would mind if I borrowed his kite. If he were here I believe that he would tell me to go ahead and fly it."

So David took Jim's kite and went to a field between the

school and his home. The kite went up and up and up, and the wind blew and blew and blew. David had never seen a kite go so high before, and he was very much excited.

And then a terrible thing happened. There were some pretty flowers in the field, and as David was holding the kite, his other hand brushed against a flower. There was a bee on the flower, and it stung him. David yelled and jumped. He let go of the string, and away sailed Jim's kite across the field and into the woods.

"Oh, oh, oh!" said David. His hand hurt, and it was puffed up from the bee sting; but his heart hurt most because he had borrowed Jim's kite without asking him, and now it was gone. David didn't know what else to do, so he went home. His mother put medicine on the bee sting, but she noticed that he was very quiet that evening. She thought it was because he had been hurt by the bee. She didn't know that David had lost Jim's kite.

The next morning David felt worse than ever. He didn't want to tell Jim that he had lost his beautiful kite. "I know what I'll do," said David; "I'll just not tell Jim. I'll let him think that someone stole the kite. Jim will never know that I took it and lost it."

But when David had decided that, he was even more unhappy. The Lord Jesus was in David's heart telling him that that was no way for a Christian to act. "You must go and tell Jim," the voice in his heart kept saying.

But David said, "No, I won't tell Jim. I'll let him think some other boy stole it."

On the way to school, David saw Jim in the road ahead of him. David's feet wanted to turn around quickly and take him the other way. But David's heart had decided something, and his heart made his feet hurry and catch up with Jim. Then David's heart made him talk. It made him say, "Jim, I borrowed your kite last night to fly it."

"Oh," said Jim, "I left it at school. I hope you had a nice time with it. Did you take it back in school?"

"No," said David. "While I was flying your kite a bee stung me, and the kite string flew out of my hand, and the kite is gone."

Jim looked very angry. He started to say something, and then suddenly he looked up into the sky. David thought maybe he was looking for his kite. Then David heard Jim say very quietly, "All right, Lord Jesus." Then to David he said, "I'm sorry that you got stung by the bee. Of course, I'm sorry that my kite was lost, too, but I can make another one."

"Aren't you awful angry?" David asked.

"No," said Jim. "I started to be, but the Lord Jesus talked to me about it, and I decided not to be. I can make another kite."

"Oh, Jim," David said, "could I help you make one? I am good at making things, and if you would tell me how, I could make one. I could give you back a kite for the lost one."

"Let's make it together!" said Jim.

So that's what David and Jim did.

Questions:

1. Why did the children at Pollybrook School like windy weather?
2. What would have happened if David had not told Jim that he lost his kite?

A Scripture verse:

Admit your faults to one another *(James 5:16)*.

A hymn to sing:

> Give of your best to the Master,
> Give of the strength of your youth;
> Throw your soul's fresh, glowing ardor
> Into the battle for truth.

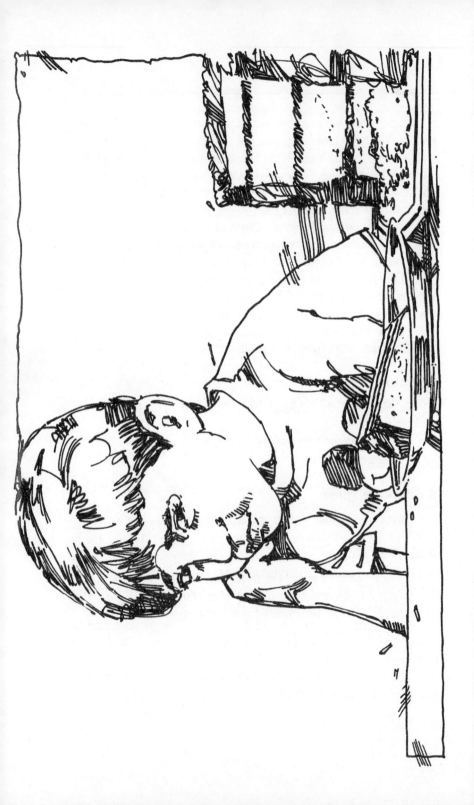

13

Jack Learns a Lesson

Jack was six years old, but sometimes he acted like a baby. He cried every time his mother asked him to help with the dishes. He cried whenever she asked him to make his bed. And he cried whenever she needed help in setting the table.

One day his mother said, "Jack, I don't enjoy hearing you cry whenever I ask you to do things. Can't you be cheerful?"

"No," said Jack, and he began to cry because he thought his mother was getting ready to ask him to dry the dishes.

One day at Sunday school the teacher talked about being kind and helpful. "That makes Jesus glad," she said, "but He is sorry when His children are selfish. Being selfish means wanting to be kind to ourselves, instead of to other people." She said that if they didn't learn to be happy when obeying their mothers and fathers, then they would find it hard to obey the Lord Jesus.

Jack thought about that. He knew he always cried instead of being cheerful when Mother needed him to help her. How could he be Jesus' helper if he wasn't Mother's helper?

"Oh, my!" Jack said. "I'd better do the dishes when Mother asks me, and not cry about it."

Jack's family went home after church and ate dinner. It was a good dinner. After dinner Mother said, "Jack, will you help wash the dishes?" And do you know what Jack did? He began to cry and cry. He forgot all about what the teacher had said.

After breakfast the next morning Jack's mother said, "Jack, will you wash the dishes?" Jack was getting ready to cry when his mother said, "No, today let's just do the things we want to do."

Jack's face brightened, and he smiled and smiled. "Don't I have to do the dishes then?" he asked hopefully.

"No," said his mother, "not unless you want to."

"Oh, boy!" said Jack. "And don't I have to go to school?"

"No, not unless you want to," said his mother.

"And can I eat the cake you made for my birthday party to-morrow?"

"Sure," said his mother, "if you want to."

Jack didn't do the dishes. He didn't go to school. For a while he played with his trains. When he got tired of that he ate four pieces of cake. Then he went outside to play, but the other children were at school. He went for a walk and came back.

"Mother," he said, "you haven't washed the dishes yet."

"Oh, no," she replied. "Today we'll just do the things we want to."

Finally it was time for lunch. Jack's mother always made good lunches for him, but today she didn't fix any lunch.

"Mother, isn't it lunchtime?" asked Jack.

"Yes," said Mother, "but I don't feel like getting lunch today, and today we're just going to do the things we like to do. Maybe you can find a glass of milk in the refrigerator."

So Jack drank the glass of milk and went out to play. But he grew tired of playing, and he was still hungry. He came back and ate four more pieces of cake and began to feel very sick.

"Mother," he said, "I feel sick. Will you help me?"

"I'm busy right now," said Mother. "Just go and lie down and perhaps you'll feel better."

By suppertime Jack felt better, but there wasn't any supper.

"Why don't you eat the rest of your birthday cake?" his mother asked. "It's your birthday tomorrow, you know."

"Oh, I don't want any more cake now," said Jack. "Will you make another cake for me tomorrow?"

"No, I don't want to do that. I want to listen to the radio."

Poor Jack! Finally he went to bed. The next morning Mother said, "Shall we do just the things we want to do today?"

Jack thought about yesterday. Even though he hadn't gone to school he hadn't had much fun at home. He remembered how sick he had felt after eating all that cake. He remembered Mother wanting to do everything else except take care of him.

"No," Jack said, "let's do things for each other today."

I guess Jack finally learned a lesson because he didn't cry any more about washing the dishes.

Questions:

1. What did Jack cry about?
2. What did his mother say that made him happy?
3. How long did he stay happy?
4. What did he decide?

A Scripture verse:

Christ didn't please Himself *(Romans 15:3)*.

A hymn to sing:

Draw me nearer, nearer, blessed Lord,
To the cross where You have died;
Draw me nearer, nearer, nearer blessed Lord,
To Your precious, bleeding side.

14

Lost in the Woods

"Say," said Billy, "what's that noise?"

"What noise?" asked Tom. "I didn't hear anything."

Both boys stopped and listened. It was so dark they couldn't see anything without using their flashlights, and the trees all around them made deep shadows. The boys were on the way home from a hike. That afternoon they had asked their mother for some sandwiches and had gone for a long walk through the woods to a neighbor's farm to play with the children there.

It was almost dark when they started back, and maybe that is why Billy kept thinking he heard funny noises. Tom didn't hear any at all.

"Come on," said Tom. "You must be just pretending you hear things, because I don't hear them. All I hear is us walking along and talking."

"No," said Billy, "I think it's probably a bear or something that wants to eat us up."

"I doubt it," Tom said. "There aren't any bears in these woods."

"Well, then, probably a lion or a tiger," said Billy.

"You're always thinking things like that, Billy. Why don't you try to think about nice things, maybe a kitten or a lost puppy or something like that? And anyway, every time we walk through here at night you think you hear things. But nothing has happened to us yet, so I don't think it will now."

"Well, anyway, I'm scared," said Billy, and he began to run down the path. Suddenly he caught his toe on a rough place on the ground, and he fell. He had been running with the flashlight in his hand and when he fell, the flashlight hit the ground hard and went out. Suddenly it was dark. Billy lay on the ground in the darkness and cried. He wasn't hurt, but he was scared.

"Oh," he sobbed, "we'll never get home. Now all kinds of things will come and eat us."

"Phooey!" said Tom. "They wouldn't want to eat a crybaby like you."

"I am not a crybaby!" said Billy, and he sat up and stopped crying. "If you're so smart, how *shall* we get home? If we try to walk we'll get off the path and get lost."

"Well," said Tom, "we'll just sit here on the path until Dad comes looking for us."

"Stay here, and get eaten up by the bears? Oh, no!" And Billy started sobbing again.

"Ah, quit being a baby!" said Tom. "Don't you know that God is taking care of us? He knows where we are. We'll get home OK. What's the use of being a Christian if you don't trust the Lord?"

"Well," said Billy, "I s-s-s-suppose you're right. Say," he said, sitting up straight, "does God always take care of Christians so they don't ever get hurt?"

"No," said Tom, "sometimes God lets them get hurt and even die, but He still is loving them and doing the best things for them."

"But I don't want to get hurt and die!" whimpered Billy.

"Maybe living in heaven would be better than you think," Tom said.

Just then the boys heard a shout, and they shouted back. Billy even quit crying. They saw a light bobbing up and down on the trail, and soon Dad's big arms were around them. They told him what had happened.

Dad said, "Well, the Lord took care of you. I guess maybe He wanted Billy to learn a lesson about trusting Him."

"Yes," said Billy, "I think so, too. I'm going to pray that He will help me trust Him and not be afraid."

Questions:

1. What made Billy afraid?
2. What happened to the flashlight?
3. Does God always keep us from getting hurt? Why not?
4. Does God love us if He lets us get hurt?

A Scripture verse:

I will trust, and not be afraid *(Isaiah 12:2,* King James Version).

A hymn to sing:

'Tis so sweet to trust in Jesus,
Just to take Him at His word;
Just to rest upon His promise;
Just to know, "Thus saith the Lord."

15

Uncle Bob's Story

Martha just loved Uncle Bob. He was kind and good, and when he came to visit he sometimes helped her do the dishes when it was her turn. Martha thought that was just perfect. Uncle Bob could tell wonderful stories, too. Usually they were stories about things that happened to him when he was a boy.

One day when Uncle Bob was visiting, Martha said, "Uncle, will you tell me a story?"

Uncle Bob said, "Sure, I'll be glad to. What kind of story do you want?"

"Oh, I don't care," said Martha, "just so it's a good story."

"I think I will tell you about a time that helped me learn to trust the Lord," Uncle Bob said.

"It happened last year. One day a letter came from the pastor of a church more than a thousand miles away from where I live. The pastor said that he wanted to have special meetings in his church, and that he wanted me to come and do the preaching.

"I was glad to do it. At the end of his letter the pastor said, 'We do not have very much money to pay you, but if you will come, we will give you $100.'

"That sounds like a lot of money," Uncle Bob said, "but when I called up the airline and asked how much it would cost to go a thousand miles and come back home, I was told that it would cost $124!"

"But that would cost too much," Martha said. "You were going to get $100. That wouldn't be enough to buy the ticket."

"That's right," said Uncle Bob. "And that bothered me because I didn't have any extra money to use. I needed my money for other things."

"Did you write and tell the man you couldn't come unless he gave you more money?" Martha wanted to know.

"No," said Uncle Bob. "I thought of doing that, but I decided I would just tell the Lord about it and ask Him what to do. After I had prayed, I believed that the Lord wanted me to go and that He would send the money some way. I wouldn't get the $100 until I had finished preaching for the pastor, so I went down to the bank and took out $124 and bought my ticket. I had a very wonderful time in the meetings, and I was very glad that I had gone. Many boys and girls, as well as their fathers and mothers, began to love the Lord Jesus and became Christians as a result of my sermons. How happy I was I had not stayed at home! Afterward the pastor gave me the $100 that had been promised and thanked me for coming.

"When it was time to leave, a man drove me to the airport. He was very happy because the Lord had helped him, through what I said, to know more about the Lord and to love and trust Him more.

"Just as I got out at the airport and was thanking the man for driving me there, he gave me an envelope. He said, 'This is my thank offering because you have helped me to know the Lord Jesus better. I want you to use what is inside the envelope for anything you need.'

"I thanked the man," Uncle Bob said, "and then went out and got on the plane. When I was seated I opened the envelope, and what do you think was in it? It was a one hundred dollar bill! I thought, *How wonderful! How good the Lord is! How well He takes care of us!* I bowed my head and closed my eyes right there on the airplane and said in my heart, 'Thank You, Lord Jesus, for helping me to trust You.' "

"Oooh!" said Martha. "If I trust the Lord will He give me $100?"

"No, probably not," said Uncle Bob, "because you don't need $100. Maybe you need to be happy even when you have to wash dishes. The Lord will make you happy if that is what you need, and He will give you $100 if that is what you need—if you trust Him. And that is the end of the story."

"Oh, thank you for telling me that story," said Martha. "I want to learn to trust Jesus too."

Questions:

1. Will the Lord give us $100 if we ask Him?
2. Why or why not?

A Scripture verse:

And it is He who will supply all your needs from His riches in glory, because of what Christ Jesus has done for us *(Philippians 4:19)*.

A hymn to sing:

Great is Your faithfulness!
Great is Your faithfulness!
Morning by morning new mercies I see;
All I have needed Your hands have provided—
Great is Your faithfulness, Lord, unto me.

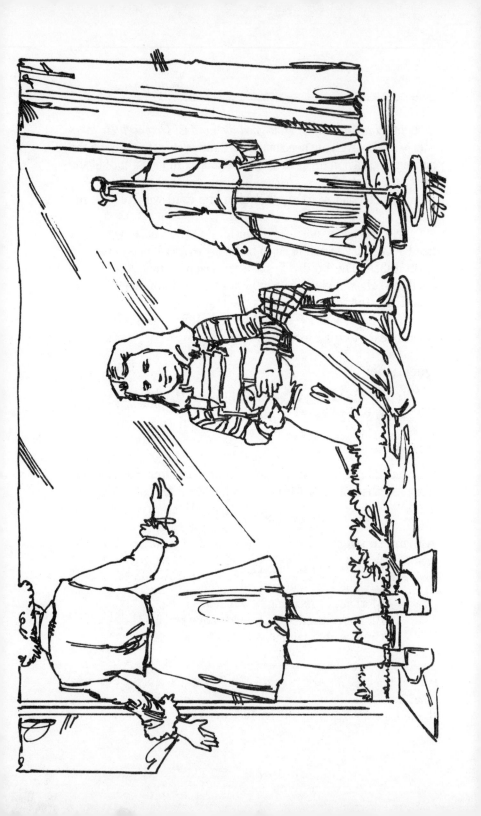

16

Treasures in Heaven

Alice lived with her father and mother and several brothers and sisters in the little house down at the end of the street. Alice's father was not well. Often he could not work and earn money to buy things for Alice and the rest of the family. They usually had enough to eat, but Alice did not have pretty clothes as so many of the other girls did. But there was one thing about Alice that was true of all the other children—she had a birthday!

And soon it would be Alice's birthday! How excited she was! One day just before her birthday there was a letter in the mailbox for her. When she opened it, what do you suppose she found? It was $25 that her Uncle Doug had sent to her for a birthday present. With the money was a letter that said Alice should use the money any way that she wished. Alice was very surprised and happy, and she began to think of all the things she could do with so much money.

She walked downtown to where the stores were and stopped in front of the dress shop. There in the window was a beautiful pink dress just her size. She could see the tag that told what size the dress was and how much it cost. The tag said that the dress cost $25. *Oh,* thought Alice excitedly, *that is just how* *much I have. What a very, very pretty dress! I can buy it with my $25.* Alice decided to buy the dress the very next day, and she ran all the way home because she was so happy.

That night when Alice was reading her Bible she happened to read a verse that said, "Lay not up for yourselves treasures on earth where moth and rust corrupt." She asked her mother what that verse meant. Her mother told her how sometimes moths get into clothes and eat big holes in them so that the dresses have to be patched and are no longer as pretty as they were and sometimes they have to be thrown away. Mother explained to Alice that Jesus meant that it was better to send our money to heaven than to use it for ourselves down here.

"Everything we buy down here," Mother said, "soon gets old, and we have to throw it away. But if we let God have the money, He will use it and give us far more beautiful things that He will keep for us until we get to heaven. Then we can have those things always and always. They never fade and never grow old."

"I would much rather have a pretty dress waiting for me in heaven that would always be pretty, instead of having a pretty dress here that would soon get old," said Alice. "How can I send $25 to heaven?"

"One way," her mother said, "is to give it to the missionaries. They will use the money to tell people about Jesus, and God will give you a prize greater than the $25 and better than a dress when you reach heaven. Whatever prize you receive will never grow old."

Alice thought about what her mother had told her. The next morning she came quickly downstairs as soon as she woke up. "Mother," she said, "I'm so glad I didn't buy that pretty dress in the shop window yesterday. I would rather give the money to the missionaries and then have a wonderful surprise waiting for me in heaven."

Questions:

1. Why was Alice glad?
2. Will Alice get a dress when she gets to heaven? Or will she get something nicer?
3. How long would the dress last if she had bought it?
4. How long will what we have in heaven last?

Some Scripture verses:

Don't store up your profits here on earth . . . but store them in heaven, where they never lose their value, and are safe from thieves *(Matthew 6:19-20)*.

A hymn to sing:

> Turn your eyes upon Jesus,
> Look full in His wonderful face;
> And the things of earth will grow strangely dim
> In the light of His glory and grace.

17

The Broken Window

"**F**irst!"
"Second!"
"Third!"

School was out for the afternoon, and the boys were getting ready to play baseball. They were deciding who would be up to bat first, who would be catcher, who would be pitcher, and so on. The ball game began, and the boys were having fun.

But all of a sudden a terrible thing happened. One of the boys hit the ball, and it went straight toward the house in the next yard. The ball sailed into a big window with a terrific crash, and the window broke into a hundred thousand pieces, sending pieces of glass all over the porch. The boys were scared. What would the owner say? What would he do to them? They didn't think about it very long. They ran away as fast as they could.

That is, some of them did. Joe and Allan didn't want to run away. They had been taught that it was wrong. So they stayed even if they were scared and wondered what was going to happen to them.

Soon the door opened, and the owner of the house came rushing out. He was excited and angry. "What's the idea of breaking my window?" he shouted. "Come over here, you two boys."

Joe and Allan went over to the man who was looking at his broken window. "Where do you boys live?" he asked. "I'm going to tell your fathers what you've done, and it's going to cost them about ten dollars to have this window replaced."

Joe and Allan looked at each other. Ten dollars! Wow! Well, one thing was sure: they didn't want their fathers to have to pay for it. That wouldn't be fair.

"Don't tell our dads," Joe said, "and we'll get the money somewhere." They told the man where they lived and started off to see where they could get ten dollars. They decided they would ask each of the boys who had been playing in the game to give seventy-five cents. They thought that then they would have enough.

The other boys were about a block away waiting for them. They laughed at Joe and Allan for not running away. And when Joe and Allan told them about the man wanting the money and explained how they could pay seventy-five cents, the boys laughed some more. "Why didn't you run away with us?" they said. "Then we wouldn't have to pay."

"Just because that wouldn't be right," said Allan. "Joe and I will pay it ourselves if you won't help us."

Joe and Allan thought a long time, but they couldn't decide how to get the ten dollars. Joe had a paper route, but he had just started it, and he didn't have five dollars for his part, although he might have it next week. The only thing Allan could think about doing was selling his bicycle. He thought he could get twenty dollars for it. Then he could pay for the broken window, and Joe could pay him the next week. Allan was very sorry to lose his bicycle, but there didn't seem to be anything else to do.

So Joe and Allan took the bicycle down to the bicycle shop, and the man paid Allan twenty dollars for it. They went back and promptly paid the man for the broken window.

When Joe and Allan went home to tell their fathers about what had happened, both fathers seemed very glad they had not run away. "Sometimes it's hard to do the right thing," Joe's father said. "But we've tried to bring you up to obey God always, no matter what happens. And we're glad that you remembered to obey God today."

Questions:

1. Why did Joe and Allan stay when the other boys ran away?
2. How did Joe and Allan each get five dollars?
3. Name those who would have been sorry if Joe and Allan had been unfair and had run away.

A Scripture verse:

We must be honest and true *(Romans 13:13)*.

A hymn to sing:

My Jesus, I love Thee, I know Thou art mine;
For You all the follies of sin I resign;
My gracious Redeemer, my Savior art Thou,
If ever I loved You, my Jesus, it's now.

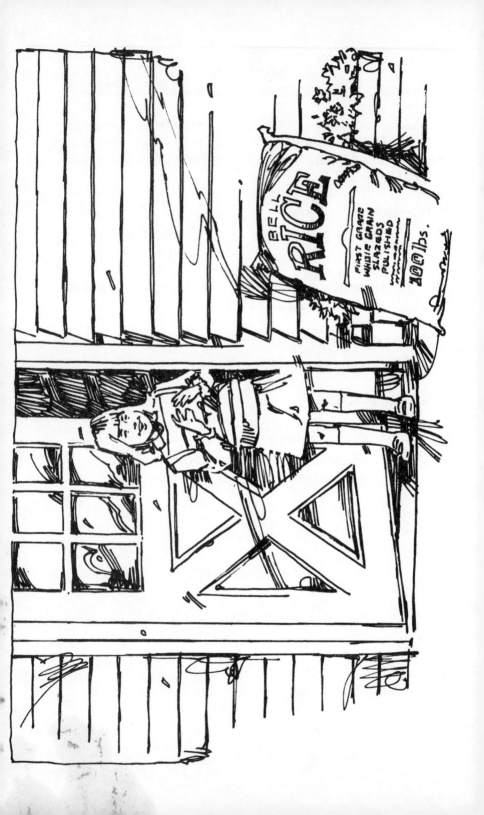

18

Surprise for Breakfast

A long time ago, across the ocean in England, there lived a man named George Mueller who had a great big house. In that house were many, many children. They were not Mr. Mueller's very own children, but they were boys and girls who didn't have any fathers or mothers to live with. Mr. Mueller had invited them to come and live with him in his big house.

One of those children was a little girl named Barbara. Barbara was six years old when she came to live with Mr. Mueller and the other children. She had a very happy time.

Mr. Mueller had told the children that he didn't have very much money to buy food for them. But he said that the Lord Jesus in heaven was taking care of them, that they need not worry, and that they ought to keep thanking the Lord Jesus because He was so kind to them.

One night after the children had their supper, Mr. Mueller said to them: "Children, all of the money is gone, and the cook tells me that there is not enough food left for our breakfast tomorrow morning. So let's pray now that the Lord Jesus will send us the food we need."

The children all got down on their knees, and Mr. Mueller led them in the prayer. He said, "Lord Jesus, You have taken care of us, and we thank You for being so kind and good to us. Now we need food for breakfast in the morning, and we ask You to send it to us. We pray in Jesus' name. Amen."

The next morning when the children awoke they ran downstairs to the breakfast table to see what the Lord Jesus had brought for them. There was nothing on their plates yet, but they sat down and waited for the cook to bring their breakfast from the kitchen.

Then Mr. Mueller came in and said, "Children, our breakfast hasn't come yet. The Lord has not sent it yet. Let's pray again."

So the children got down on their knees again, and Mr. Mueller prayed that the Lord would send them the food that they needed.

Then Mr. Mueller said to the children, "Now, children, you may run out and play. It may be that the Lord does not want us to have breakfast this morning, but He will surely provide our needs as He always has."

Just as the children were getting ready to leave the table there was a knock at the front door. Mr. Mueller said, "Barbara, you may go and see who is there and what is wanted."

Barbara ran to the door and opened it, and who do you think was there? Nobody! Someone had been there but had gone. He had left a great big bag of rice. Barbara ran into the house. "Oh," she cried, "there is a bag, a great big bag of rice for our breakfast, waiting on the porch!"

"Where is the man who brought it to us?" asked Mr. Mueller. "We must thank him."

"There was no one there," said Barbara. "I think perhaps an angel brought it."

"That might easily be," said Mr. Mueller. "Or perhaps someone ran away after leaving it, so we wouldn't know who it was. But it was the Lord who sent it, so let us kneel again and thank Him for sending our breakfast."

And that is just what the children did.

Many times after that the children learned how the Lord Jesus took care of them.

And the Lord is ready to answer our prayers today, too, just as He did for Mr. Mueller and the children in the big house long ago.

Questions:

1. Did Mr. Mueller have enough money to buy food for the children?
2. Do you think that when the children needed food a sack of rice was *always* left at the door? What other ways might God use to give them food?
3. Has God ever answered a prayer of yours? Does He like to answer our prayers?

A Scripture verse:

Don't worry about anything: instead, pray about everything; tell God your needs *(Philippians 4:6)*.

A hymn to sing:

Jesus loves me! this I know,
For the Bible tells me so;
Little ones to Him belong;
They are weak, but He is strong.
Yes, Jesus loves me, yes, Jesus loves me,
Yes, Jesus loves me—the Bible tells me so.

19

An Answer to Prayer

It was gone. Yes, it was gone. The dollar had been right in Susan's hand while she was walking along the sidewalk to the store. She had stopped to talk to Sarah a minute, but she hadn't been playing, and now the dollar wasn't in her hand.

Susan walked slowly back toward home, looking at the sidewalk and looking in the grass at the edge of the sidewalk on both sides. But she couldn't find the dollar anywhere. Then Susan turned around and walked back again slowly to where she first noticed that the dollar was lost, but she still couldn't find it.

Susan felt like crying, but she knew that wouldn't help. She didn't want to go back and ask Mother for another dollar to buy the quart of milk. Mother would think that she was very careless, and she might even be angry and scold her.

Susan didn't know what to do, so she went back to talk to Sarah. "Sarah," she said, "I've lost the dollar that I had in my hand. I've looked all over, and I can't find it anywhere. And now I don't know what to do."

"Oh, I'm sorry," said Sarah. "I'll help you look for it." So Sarah and Susan both looked and looked. They looked on the sidewalk, in the cracks in the sidewalk, and in the grass on both sides. They even looked in the street. They asked everyone who came along whether he had seen a dollar. But no one had.

Finally they sat down under the shade of a tree by the sidewalk to rest and to think.

"I know one other thing you might do before we have to go and tell your mother," said Sarah.

"Oh, what is that?" asked Susan.

"We can pray and ask God to help us find it," Sarah said. "God knows just where the dollar is; and if He wants to He can show us just where it is, if we ask Him."

"Wouldn't He show us unless we asked Him?" Susan wanted to know.

"He might," Sarah said, "but He hasn't. Even if we ask Him He might not want us to find it, but at least we can try."

So Sarah and Susan sat there under the tree, and each one prayed. Susan said, "Dear God, I have lost my dollar. Please help me to find it."

And Sarah prayed, "Dear God, Susan has lost her dollar. Please help us to find it if it is Your will." Sarah's mother had told her once that when God doesn't give us the things we ask for, it is better that we don't have them, no matter how much we want them.

Just as Sarah and Susan finished their prayers, Susan gave a little cry and jumped up. She had put her hand in the pocket of her dress—and now, out came the dollar!

"Oh," said Susan, "just as we were praying, I thought about feeling in my pocket to see if I had put it there. I don't know why I didn't think of that before. I guess we didn't need to pray about it after all, because it was in my pocket all the time."

"Oh, no!" Sarah said, laughing. "That isn't the way to think about it. That is the way God answered your prayer. He made you think about where you put it. That is a very, very nice answer to our prayer."

"Yes," said Susan, "a very nice answer, and now I think we should sit down again and thank God for giving my dollar back to me."

And that is just what they did. Then Susan ran to the store and brought the milk and hurried home to tell Mother what had happened and how God had answered their prayer.

Questions:

1. What was Susan going to do with the dollar?
2. Where did she and Sarah look for the money?
3. How did God answer their prayer?
4. Will God always help us find lost money? Why or why not?

A Scripture verse:

Always keep on praying *(1 Thessalonians 5:17)*.

A hymn to sing:

O worship the King, all glorious above,
O gratefully sing His power and His love;
Our Shield and Defender, the Ancient of Days,
Pavilioned in splendor, and girded with praise.

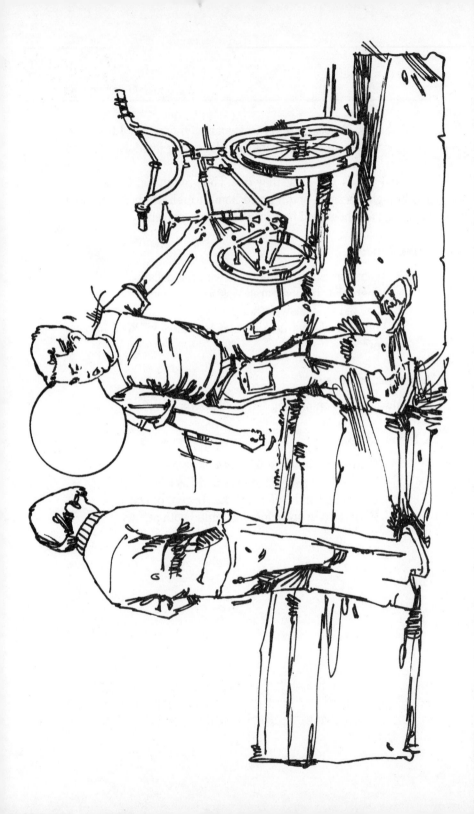

20

The Angry Boy

Allan was angry. He was sure it was all George's fault, and he told George so. "You borrowed my bike and then you ran over a tack and the tire is flat. Now the bicycle is no good!"

"I'll fix the tire," said George, "and then the bike will be as good as new."

"It won't either," said Allan. "It will still be just an old bicycle with a patched tire. It's all your fault."

Just then Mother came to the door. "What is the matter, Allan?" she called.

"George wrecked my bike," Allan said. "He has to get me a new one. I never want to play with him again." He turned to George. "I hate you. You old bike-wrecker!" he said.

"But Allan," said Mother, "how can George buy you a new bike, or even fix the tire when you have just killed him?"

"Killed him!" exclaimed Allan. "I haven't even punched him on the nose like I should."

"No," said Mother, "but you wanted to, and the Bible says that if we want to do a wicked or wrong thing, in God's sight it is as though we had done it. If we are angry with someone, we would really like to hurt him, and in God's sight it is as though we had killed him, and God will judge us. God is not at all pleased with you now."

Allan was so angry with George and so surprised by what Mother had just told him that he didn't know what to do. He ran out into the yard crying.

George said, "I'm sorry I ran over the tack, Mother, but I couldn't help it. I'll fix the bike now."

"All right," said Mother. "That's probably the best thing to do."

"Mother," said George, "is Allan not a Christian now, because he is angry?"

"I think he is a Christian," said Mother, "but he has let his anger get a grip on him instead of letting Jesus tend to it as only Jesus can. I think he still loves the Lord Jesus, although he is doing wrong by being angry. We must pray for him to tell God that he is sorry."

That night the supper table was not a very happy place, and Allan went to bed as soon as he could. He felt terrible. He didn't know what to do. He knew that God was displeased and grieved with him.

After he had gone to bed, Father came up to talk with him. "Allan," he said, "don't you know what to do when you have done something wrong?"

"Yes," said Allan, "I say I am sorry."

"Yes," said Father, "and also you should tell God that you are sorry and ask Him to help you to be truly sorry. Remember the verse in the Bible that says that if we confess our sins He will forgive us?"

Allan got down on his knees beside his bed with Father and said, "Lord Jesus, I am sorry that I was angry with George."

Then Allan did an even harder thing. He went downstairs and found George and said, "George, I'm sorry I got mad."

George said, "Aw, that's OK," and all of a sudden Allan felt better. God had forgiven him, and George had forgiven him.

"Thank You," he said in his heart to the Lord Jesus, "for forgiving me, and please help me not to be angry again when I shouldn't be."

Questions:

1. What had George done to Allan's bike?
2. What did Mother mean when she said Allan had "killed" George?
3. What two things did Allan do that made everything all right again?

A Scripture verse:

If you are only angry, even in your own home, you are in danger of judgment *(Matthew 5:22)*.

A hymn to sing:

> Draw me nearer, nearer, blessed Lord,
> To the cross where You have died;
> Draw me nearer, nearer, nearer, blessed Lord,
> To Your precious, bleeding side.

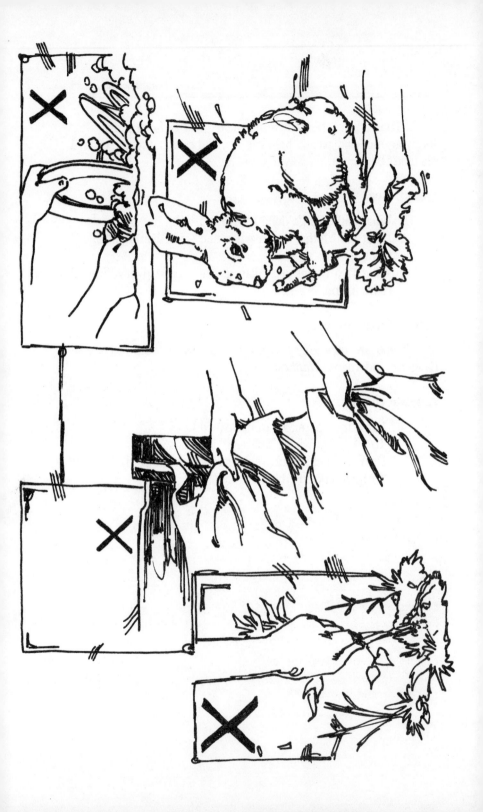

21

Doing Chores

Keith could never remember to do the things he was supposed to do. He forgot to feed his pet rabbits, forgot to make his
bed, forgot to put away his clothes, forgot when it was his turn to
help with the dishes, and he forgot to take care of his garden. He
had planted some beets in the spring, and now it was hard to find
the beets because there were so many weeds.

"Oh, Mother," Keith would say when she reminded him
about taking care of the garden, "I need to go out and play now. I
don't like to pull weeds. Besides, there are so many of them I
couldn't pull them all out today."

Then Mother had an idea. She said, "Keith, how would you
like to make a chart?"

"What is a chart?" Keith asked.

"A chart is a piece of paper with lines and words on it,"
Mother explained. "This chart that I am talking about would help
you to remember about doing your chores, and it also would help
to get your garden weeded."

"How could a piece of paper with lines on it ever do that?"
Keith wanted to know.

"I'll show you," Mother said.

Keith got a piece of paper and a pencil and a ruler, and Mother put some lines and words on the piece of paper.

"Now," said Mother, "all you have to do is put an X every time you do one of the jobs. When you feed the rabbits this evening, put an X in the square that is opposite Monday evening. Tomorrow morning when you feed the rabbits, put an X in the Tuesday morning square."

"Yes," said Keith, "I see how to do it. And when I do the dishes I'll put an X in that square. And when I make the bed I'll put an X in the right square. But what does it mean where it says 'weed two feet?' Are my feet weedy?"

Mother laughed. "No," she said, "Your feet are all right as long as they carry you out to the garden. That means that you ought to weed part of the row every day instead of trying to do all of the row at once. If you could weed about two feet every day, you would soon have it done."

"How far is two feet?" Keith asked. "About this far?" and he put out his hands to show his mother how much he meant.

"Yes," said Mother, "just about that far. If you'll do that much every day, by the end of the week you'll have the full row weeded."

"That shouldn't be hard," said Keith. "I could do that much in about ten minutes."

"I think you can," said Mother. "Now why don't you start filling in the chart?"

So Keith ran downstairs and fed his rabbits and ran indoors to put an X on the chart. Then he ran over to the sink and dried all the dishes and ran back and put an X on the chart. Then he ran upstairs to make his bed and then ran downstairs to put an X on the chart. Then he ran out to the garden, and in about six minutes came back and put an X on the chart.

"Why, Keith," his mother asked, "is that all the time it took to take care of your garden?"

"Yes," said Keith, "it was very easy. I think I weeded about three feet instead of two."

"Good," said Mother. "And was it hard work?"

"No," said Keith, "it is easy to do a little at a time. And I did a good job. All of the weeds are out of the part I did. Tomorrow I think I will do four feet instead of two feet. I am a big boy, and I can do more than you thought."

And do you know what happened? Next morning, when Keith went out to weed his row of beets, he decided he was going to do the whole row. He worked and worked and took one weed at a time, and pretty soon he got right up to the end of the row. He was very happy and ran to tell Mother. And Mother was very happy, too.

Would you like to make a chart to help you remember to do the things Mother wants you to do? Why don't you try it tomorrow morning and see how it works?

Questions:

1. Did Keith have a good memory?
2. How did his mother help him to remember?
3. Was his garden weeded when Keith tried to do it all at once? How did the weeding become easy?

A Scripture verse:

Whatever your hand finds to do, do it with your might *(Ecclesiastes 9:10, The Amplified Bible)*.

A hymn to sing:

Work, for the night is coming,
Work through the morning hours;
Work while the dew is sparkling;
Work 'mid springing flowers.
Work when the day grows brighter,
Work in the glowing sun;
Work, for the night is coming,
When your work is done.

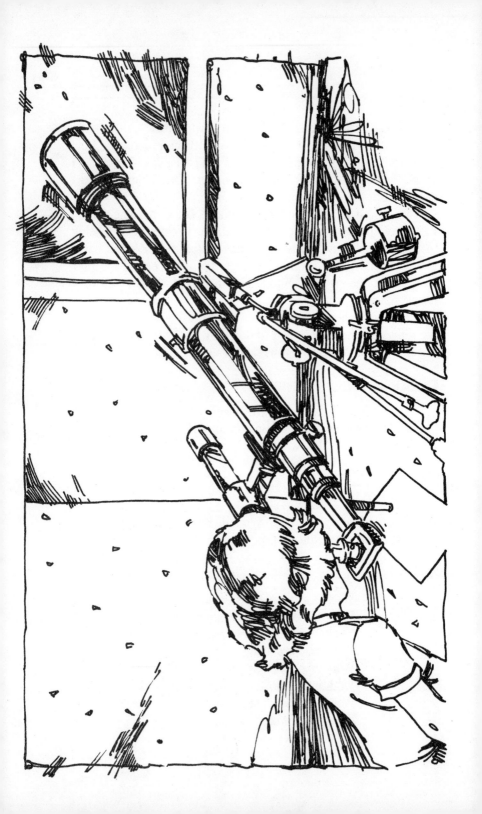

22

The Eclipse of the Moon

Jane was in her pajamas when the telephone rang, and her mother answered it. After she had talked a little while, her mother hung up the receiver. Jane could tell right away that something exciting was going to happen.

Mother said, "Jane, how would you like to stay up late tonight? Mr. Burton has asked us to come over and look at the moon through his big telescope."

"Oh, good!" said Jane. "I like Mr. Burton and his telescope. It's fun to look through the telescope and see the things in the sky. Why does he want us to look at the moon?"

"There is going to be an eclipse of the moon tonight," Jane's mother said, "and Mr. Burton thought that we would like to see it."

"What is an eclipse of the moon?" Jane didn't know.

Mother said, "You hurry and get dressed, and we'll ask Mr. Burton the questions."

Pretty soon Jane went with her mother and daddy to a little house in Mr. Burton's backyard. The top of the little house was round. It was fixed so that it could open and Mr. Burton's telescope could look up right through the roof into the sky. Mr. Burton pointed the telescope at the moon.

At first when Jane looked she couldn't believe that she was looking at the moon because it wasn't round and shiny like the moon at all. Instead she seemed to be looking at big mountains and valleys. When she told Mr. Burton about it he said, "Why, you *are* looking at mountains and valleys. Those are mountains on the moon. The telescope brings us so close to the moon that we can't see all of it at once."

Soon Jane noticed that one side of the moon was getting dark. Mr. Burton explained that the earth was making a great big shadow that was spreading over the moon. Soon the moon would be almost all dark because the shadow of the earth would cover it.

"Now I know what an eclipse of the moon is," said Jane.

"Well," said Mr. Burton, "it is very wonderful, but very scary if you don't know what is happening. The Indians used to think that some evil spirit was taking the moon away, whenever they saw the shadow creeping over it like this."

"I don't think an evil spirit could take the moon away. Do you, Mr. Burton?" asked Jane.

"No, indeed," said Mr. Burton. "God made the moon to be there, and it will always stay there until He decides to take it away."

"Will He take it away some day?" questioned Jane.

"Well," said Mr. Burton, "the Bible says that the heaven and the earth will go away some day and there will be a new heaven and a new earth instead. There are many things we do not understand, but it certainly sounds like the moon is going to disappear sometime."

"But how did the moon get there in the first place?" Jane asked.

Then Mr. Burton explained that the Lord Jesus Christ had made the moon and the earth and the sun and had put the stars in the heavens billions and billions of miles away from the earth.

Jane thought, *How great God must be!* Then she asked, "Mr. Burton, is there any special day to celebrate when Jesus made everything? We have a special day for the Fourth of July and a special day for Christmas. Is there a special Creation Day too?"

"No," said Mr. Burton, "but that would be a good idea."

"Well, wait a minute," he exclaimed. "Of course there is! Do you remember how God made all things in six days and rested the seventh day because all of His work was completed? Saturday is Creation Day. That is the day when we ought to remember that God made everything."

The next Saturday morning when Jane jumped out of bed, she ran to her mother and said, "Mother, do you know what day this is?"

"Yes," said Mother. "It's Saturday."

"It is Saturday," said Jane, "but it is Creation Day too."

"So it is," said Mother as she kissed her. "All day today let's think about how great God is."

Questions:

1. How does the moon appear through a telescope?
2. What is an eclipse?
3. Do we have a special Creation Day?

A Scripture verse:

The heavens are telling the glory of God *(Psalm 19:1).*

A hymn to sing:

> This is my Father's world,
> And to my listening ears
> All nature sings, and 'round me rings
> The music of the spheres.

23

An Exciting Adventure

"**C**ome on, come on," said Lou Ann. "Let's pick some wild flowers in the field back of the house."

All the children thought that was a fine idea, and off they went in the warm summer sunshine. Peter, who was already five years old, wanted to go ahead and act as leader, and so did Jerry. Jerry was almost seven and thought he should be leader because he was the oldest.

"Well," said Lou Ann, "let Peter lead when we go, and Jerry can lead on the way back."

That idea made everybody happy, so that is what they did.

But first Lou Ann remembered to tell Mother where they were going. She knew Mother would let them go, but Mother always wanted to know where her three children were playing.

"You go on ahead, and I'll tell Mother and catch up," said Lou Ann.

So off went Peter and Jerry with a basket to put the flowers in. They knew how happy Daddy would be to see the pretty flowers on the supper table when he got home from work.

Lou Ann found Mother, and she said they could go while she went to the store.

Lou Ann ran to catch up. The others were watching for her, and when they saw her coming they waved and went on more slowly.

Peter was the first to notice something was wrong. "Where's Lou Ann?" he asked.

Both boys turned around to look, but Lou Ann wasn't there. "That's funny," said Jerry. "She was there just a moment ago. Maybe she's hiding, only there isn't anywhere to hide."

"Let's go back," said Peter.

So they did.

"Listen," said Jerry, "I think I heard Lou Ann calling us."

They all stopped and listened. It was Lou Ann, but her voice seemed to be coming from somewhere underneath their feet.

"Lou Ann," yelled Peter, "where are you?"

"Here," said Lou Ann's voice. "I fell into a hole, and I can't get out."

"Oh, dear," said Jerry. "How shall we find the hole?" And then he saw it just about two feet ahead of him. If he hadn't stopped quickly he would have walked right into it just as Lou Ann had done.

Jerry and Peter both got down on their stomachs and looked. The hole was round, and its iron top was lying nearby almost hidden in the grass. Somebody had taken it off for some reason and had forgotten to put it back on.

At first they couldn't see anything at all down inside the hole because it was dark, but just then they heard Lou Ann say, "Please get me out. I'm scared, and I hurt myself when I fell, and it's cold."

Then the boys could see Lou Ann standing in some water about ten feet below them.

"Wow!" said Peter.

"Oh, dear," said Jerry, "how can we get her out? I'd better run and get Mother."

"No, she isn't home," said Lou Ann. "She's gone to the store." And then Lou Ann began to cry.

Jerry was thinking and thinking, but he couldn't think of any way to get Lou Ann out of the deep hole. Then all of a sudden he had the best idea.

"Oh," he said, "I know what to do. Remember what Daddy read to us in the Bible last night in family prayers about asking God what to do when we need help? I think we should ask Him right now."

"Oh, yes, let's!" said Lou Ann.

And Peter said, "You pray first, Jerry, because you're oldest."

So Jerry said, "Dear God, we can't get Lou Ann out, and she is cold, and Mother isn't home. Will You help us?"

And Peter said, "Dear God, please help us because we don't know what to do."

And Lou Ann down in the water said, "Dear God, please help them to get me out, because I'm cold and scared, but I know You are here with me, and I shouldn't be scared." Then Lou Ann started to cry again, although she tried hard not to.

All of a sudden Peter said, "I know what to do. I started to think about it while we were praying. Let's get Daddy's ladder out of the garage. We should have thought of that before."

"Oh, no," said Lou Ann. "Don't leave me here all alone!" Then all of a sudden she stopped crying. "I'll be all right," she said. "I just thought of the Bible verse I learned last Sunday. It says, 'I will trust and not be afraid.' "

Jerry and Peter ran as fast as they could and found the ladder. It was hard work carrying it, because it was big and heavy. But they finally got back, and Lou Ann was so glad to see them she almost started crying again.

That night Daddy said he couldn't see how they got the ladder into the hole. Jerry told him, "I think God was helping us because otherwise it might have slipped and fallen right on Lou Ann."

Anyway Lou Ann was soon out. The children went home very tired, and Lou Ann was all wet and muddy.

Mother got home from the store about that time. She said, "Let's pray now and thank God for helping you know what to do." So Mother and the children all knelt down in the kitchen.

Mother and the boys prayed first. Then Lou Ann said, "Thank You, God, for helping us. I'm almost glad I fell in the hole, because now we all know more about praying and how You help us."

Questions:

1. Why wasn't Lou Ann with the other children?
2. How did the children think of a way to get Lou Ann out?
3. Did they remember to thank God afterward?

A Scripture verse:

Let Him have all your worries and cares, for He is always thinking about you and watching everything that concerns you *(1 Peter 5:7).*

A hymn to sing:

> I'm a child of the King,
> A child of the King:
> With Jesus my Saviour,
> I'm a child of the King.

24

Growing Up

John was feeling bad. He didn't know what the trouble was, but he didn't want to play, and he didn't want to read, and he didn't want to do much of anything.

"Mother," he said, "I wish I didn't have to be a child. I wish I was a grown-up so that I could do lots of things."

"What kind of things?" Mother wanted to know.

"Oh," he said, "lots of things. I would know what I was going to do when I grow up, and I would know who I was going to marry, and I would get to go to other parts of the country and see what they are like. Mother," he said, "I know who I would like to marry when I grow up. I would like to marry Judy."

"Judy is a very nice girl," Mother said, "but I am afraid that Judy doesn't know much about the Lord Jesus. If she is not a Christian, you could never marry her and be happy with her, or with anyone else who is not a Christian."

"Why must I marry a Christian?" John wanted to know. "If the person I wanted to marry is nice, wouldn't that be all right? Even if she doesn't know the Lord Jesus?"

"No," said Mother, "it doesn't work out very well. When people who love the Lord Jesus marry people who don't love Him, they are never very happy. Do you know why?"

John thought a minute. "Well," he said, "probably it would be because I would always be wanting to do what the Bible says, and the other person wouldn't want to, but would want to do something else. Then we would be unhappy because we would have to do different things."

"Yes," said Mother, "that is just what happens."

"But wouldn't the person who wasn't a Christian become a Christian when she married someone who loved the Lord Jesus?" John wanted to know.

"Lots of times that is what Christians think when they marry those who do not love the Lord," said Mother. "But usually it doesn't happen that way. Usually the person who isn't a Christian laughs so much at the other person that after they have been married a little while the other person stops loving the Lord as much as he did before. He doesn't feel like praying and reading the Bible anymore because the other person thinks that is very foolish. And because the other person likes to do things that Jesus wouldn't like, the Christian begins doing those things too. So instead of the person who isn't a Christian becoming one, usually the person who is a Christian becomes a very poor one."

"Does the Bible teach that it is all right to marry people who aren't Christians?" John asked.

Mother said, "There is a verse in the Bible that says, 'Be not unequally yoked together with unbelievers.' That means that we must not marry unbelievers—non-Christians. So if anyone does, he is disobeying God."

"Then I have decided not to marry Judy when I grow up," John said, "because I am going to obey the Word of God. Unless Judy becomes really and truly a Christian. And even then, maybe by the time I am grown up I will want to marry someone else instead."

Mother smiled a little smile. "That may very well be," she said. "But meanwhile we will pray for Judy."

Questions:

1. When a Christian girl or boy grows up, should he or she marry a person who isn't a Christian?
2. When that happens, will the other person usually become a Christian?
3. Why would it be hard to be a good Christian when married to a person who doesn't love the Lord Jesus? Would it be hard or easy to pray?
4. What did John decide?

A Scripture verse:

She may marry again, but only if she marries a Christian *(1 Corinthians 7:39)*.

A hymn to sing:

>Trust and obey,
>For there's no other way
>To be happy in Jesus,
>But to trust and obey.

25

Grandpa Jenkins Goes Home

Grandpa Jenkins especially loved Patty and Jan, because they were his very own grandchildren. Patty and Jan loved Grandpa because he was their very own grandpa. When he came to visit he would always tell them a story just before they went to bed, and the stories he told were the very best stories that there ever were.

Patty and Jan had been excited all day because Grandpa was going to visit them again. They were going with Daddy after supper to the airport. Patty and Jan couldn't seem to eat very much, and finally Daddy said, "All right, girls, get in the car and let's go find Grandpa Jenkins." Mother waved good-bye to them and stayed home to take care of the baby.

Away they went to the airport. At exactly ten minutes after six by Daddy's wristwatch, the big plane arrived. Sure enough, there was Grandpa with his cane, his bag, and his smile. Patty and Jan almost knocked him off his feet because they were so glad to see him. Father took Grandpa's bag, and they all went back to the car with everyone happily talking at once.

As soon as Grandpa got home and had kissed Mother and talked a little while, he said he would like to go to bed.

Patty said, "If you are tired, perhaps you would rather not tell us a story tonight. Could you tell us a story in the morning instead, right after breakfast?"

"Now, maybe that would be a good idea," said Grandpa. "I am pretty tired tonight, and if you little girls will let me do it that way, I'll tell you a story the first thing after breakfast."

Grandpa smiled and said good night to everyone and went off to bed.

When Patty and Jan woke up the next morning, they dressed and ran down to see if Grandpa was waiting for them. Mother and Daddy were in the kitchen, but Grandpa wasn't there. They could tell that Mother had been crying.

"Where's Grandpa?" Patty and Jan wanted to know. "Isn't he up yet? We are ready for our story."

Mother said, "Come here, girls, and let me talk to you for a little while." Patty and Jan went over and stood by their mother. "Children," said Mother, "Grandpa isn't here. The angels came last night and took Grandpa to heaven to be with Jesus."

Patty and Jan were very much surprised. "Will he be gone very long?" they asked. "He was going to tell us a story."

Mother smiled just a little bit. "Grandpa is going to stay with Jesus," she said. "We shall miss him here, but he was very glad that it was time for him to go. During the night he called me and said that he was quite sure that he was going to die. He told me how much he loved the Lord Jesus and how much Jesus had done for him all his life, and pretty soon he went to sleep. While he was asleep the angels came for him and took him away."

"Did you see the angels?" Jan wanted to know.

"No," said Father. "Grandpa's body is still up in his bedroom. The angels came to get his spirit. The real Grandpa is with Jesus, while his old body, which he doesn't need anymore, is left behind."

Father took Patty and Jan up to Grandpa's room, and they could see what seemed like Grandpa asleep, but it wasn't Grandpa at all. It was just Grandpa's body. Grandpa had gone up to heaven. Father explained that soon a long black car would come and take Grandpa's body where they would take care of it until the funeral.

"What is a funeral?" the children questioned.

"The funeral is a service at the church that Grandpa's friends and loved ones will come to. The pastor will talk about Grandpa and how he loved Jesus and how he is in heaven with Jesus now. Then they will take Grandpa's body to the cemetery and bury it in the ground. Some day when Jesus comes back for all His people, Grandpa's body, and the bodies of all the other Christians who have died, will come back to life. Grandpa doesn't need his body now, but Jesus wants him to have it later on. Only then it will be a different kind of body, and it will never be sick and never die."

"I'm sorry that Grandpa has gone away," said Patty, "but I'm glad that he is with Jesus."

Jan said, "I am glad and sad at the same time. Most of all I am glad that Grandpa is so happy now, and he isn't tired anymore."

Questions:

1. Why did Patty and Jan love to have Grandpa visit them?
2. Why didn't Grandpa tell them a story in the morning?
3. What happened to Grandpa's body?
4. Where was Grandpa?

A Scripture verse:

And we are not afraid, but are glad to be rid of these bodies, for then we will be at home with the Lord *(2 Corinthians 5:8).*

A hymn to sing:

> When we all get to heaven,
> What a day of rejoicing that will be!
> When we all see Jesus,
> We'll sing and shout the victory.

26

The Garden in the Weeds

Peter Miller was more excited than he could ever remember being in all his life before. Today the Millers were moving to a new home out in the country. Peter had never seen the new home, but his father had told him all about it. It was a big house with a big porch on which he could ride his tricycle. It had a wood-shed, and a garage for Peter's brothers and sisters to put their bicycles in. It had a real barn for horses and cows to live in, and it had a special little house for chickens. Best of all, Daddy was going to buy a pet rabbit for Peter.

Tim, Peter's big brother, was in the fifth grade. "Don't be so excited," Tim said. But Peter just wiggled and jumped and squirmed some more.

Pretty soon Father said, "All right, children, all right, Mother, let's all get into the car and go to our new home."

Peter didn't know how it happened, but after he got in the car he went to sleep! He slept and he slept, and the car went and went. Just as Peter woke up, the car was turning into the drive-way of the new house. When Peter looked out the car window, there was a great big house and the barn and the chicken house and the garage. He could see the pen his father had made for his pet rabbit, and there was the rabbit in the pen eating grass!

Peter's excitement grew bigger and bigger, and he jumped out of the car and ran around the house looking at everything.

Tim said, "Come on, Peter, let's go back of the barn and see what is in the field." In back of the barn all they could see was high grass and weeds, much higher than Peter's head.

"That's funny," Tim said to Peter. "Wonder where all these weeds came from?" He began to look around under the weeds, and soon he said, "Come here, Peter, and see what I've found." Peter came rushing over and Tim showed him a nice red tomato that he had just picked off the tomato plant under the weeds.

"I think this must have been a garden that someone forgot to take care of. The weeds have grown so tall that it is hard to find the garden plants," Tim exclaimed. "Let's look some more."

They did, and soon Peter found another tomato plant, then another and another. After a while they found some bean plants growing under the weeds and then some corn and squash. All the garden plants were very small because the weeds had grown so big that the good plants hadn't had a chance to grow.

Tim and Peter worked for about an hour, pulling up weeds and carrying them to the side of the field. When they were through, a whole row of tomato plants could be seen where the weeds had been.

Then they went to tell Father about it.

"That's fine," Father said. "When I looked back of the barn all I saw was weeds. I never thought that underneath there would be any good things to eat. It is a good thing you boys found the garden now, or all the tomatoes would have spoiled."

"Say," said Mother, "I think we could learn a lesson from this. Did you boys know that our hearts are like gardens?"

"No," said Peter. "Is my heart like a garden?"

"Sure," said Tim, because he knew lots of things that Peter didn't know. "When we ask Jesus to be our Savior, He comes into our hearts, and God takes away the weeds."

"That's right," said Father. "God plants seeds of happiness and kindness, and many other wonderful seeds in our hearts. The seeds grow up into fine, strong plants that grow happiness instead of tomatoes. But if we don't take care of the new garden by asking Jesus to help keep the weeds out, pretty soon we can hardly find the good plants that Jesus put there."

"What kind of weeds grow in our hearts?" Peter asked.

Tim said, "I think our sins are the weeds. If we tell a lie and don't ask Jesus to forgive us, that is a great big weed. Soon a lot of weeds grow near it, and then the good plants can't grow."

"That's right," Father said. "When you do something wrong, ask Jesus to forgive you. Then the weed won't be there anymore, because He will pull it out. When we read our Bibles and pray and do what Jesus says, that is the way we water the good seeds. Then we will have a lovely garden in our hearts for Jesus to walk in."

Questions:

1. What did the boys see at first behind the barn?
2. Why were the good plants so small?
3. What are the weeds in our hearts, and how do we get rid of them?

A Scripture verse:

But if we confess our sins to Him, He can be depended on to forgive us our sins and to cleanse us from every wrong *(1 John 1:9).*

A hymn to sing:

> Just now, your doubtings give o'er;
> Just now, reject Him no more;
> Just now, throw open the door;
> Let Jesus come into your heart.

27

A Wonderful Visit

"**N**ext Sunday," said Miss Ruth to the children as they were getting ready to go home from Sunday school, "we're going to meet here just as we usually do, and then we are going to visit the pastor's study."

"What is the pastor's study?" Nancy asked.

"I know," said Todd. "The pastor's study is the room where he has his books and where he reads his Bible and prays and gets ready to preach his sermons on Sunday mornings."

"That's right, Todd," said Miss Ruth, "and he has invited us to come and see it. Would you like to go?"

"Oh, yes," said Todd. "I would like to go. Someday I would like to be a pastor if the Lord wants me to, and I would like to know how to preach a sermon."

The next Sunday the children left their Sunday school room and walked quietly to the back of the church building. There, holding the door open for them was Pastor Smith. "Good morning, children," he said. "Thank you for coming to visit me. Come in and see my study."

The children said, "Good morning, Pastor Smith. We are glad you invited us to come and see your study."

The children went into the pastor's study. It was a small room, and it had many books on shelves along the walls. It had a study table and a lamp and a big chair.

"This is where I read my Bible and pray and think about what God wants me to preach on Sunday," said Pastor Smith.

"How can you pray in such a little room?" Todd questioned. "We pray in our Sunday school class, and it is a bigger room than this. And I pray in my bedroom at home before I go to bed, and it is bigger than this."

"Oh," said the pastor, "the size of the room doesn't make any difference! We can pray in a big room or in a little room."

"Do you pray very much?" Todd wanted to know.

"Oh, yes, quite a bit," said Pastor Smith. "I have to pray about you children, about your mothers and daddies, about our missionaries, about the people in our city who aren't Christians, about myself, and about many other things."

"How do you remember all the things you want to pray about?" asked one of the children.

"I keep a little notebook," said the pastor, and he showed them a notebook among his books. He took it down and opened it, and they could see that it had pages of writing. "I made a list of things I want to pray for, and I pray for some of them every day. That way I don't forget."

When Todd got home from church, he was still thinking about Pastor Smith's list of things to pray about. "I'm going to make a list of things to pray about," said Todd to his father. "Will you give me a piece of paper and a pencil?"

"Yes," said Todd's father. "That's a good idea."

So Todd made a list. He put down, "Father, Mother, sister, Mr. and Mrs. Jones in Africa," and several other names. When he had finished, he had fourteen things that he wanted to pray about. "Every night when I go to bed," Todd said, "I will pray about at least two of these things."

And he did.

Questions:

1. What is a study?
2. Can we pray and read the Bible if we don't have a study?
3. What is a prayer list?

A Scripture verse:

Pray all the time. Ask God for anything in line with the Holy Spirit's wishes *(Ephesians 6:18)*.

A hymn to sing:

Sweet hour of prayer, sweet hour of prayer,
That calls me from a world of care,
And bids me at my Father's throne
Make all my wants and wishes known.

28

What Shall I Do When I Grow Up?

Four boys were talking about what they were going to be when they grew up.

Edward said, "I am going to be an airplane pilot."

Jim said, "I am going to be a minister and preach the gospel."

Harold said, "I am going to be a doctor."

Doug didn't say anything.

"What are you going to be?" the three boys asked him.

Doug looked sad. "I don't know what I want to be. Sometimes I think I want to be a fireman, and sometimes I think I want to be a doctor. Sometimes I think I want to be a farmer, and sometimes I think a lot of other things. But I am never sure."

The three boys looked sad too. They thought that Doug ought to know what he was going to be when he grew up.

Pretty soon Doug's big sister Carla came along. "Why are you boys looking so sorry?" she wanted to know.

"We are sorry because Doug doesn't know what to be when he grows up," the boys told her. "Do you know what he ought to be?"

"No," Carla said, "but perhaps we should go ask the pastor. Perhaps he will know." So the five children went over to see the pastor.

He was very glad to see them. "Come right in, children," he said, "and sit on these chairs. What can I do for you?"

Then they told him about Doug and how he didn't know what he was going to be when he grew up and how the other three boys had already decided. They wanted to know what Doug should be.

"You boys are asking me a hard question," the pastor said. "I think Doug should be whatever God wants him to be. I don't think he would want to be anything else."

"But how can I find out what God wants me to be?" Doug asked.

The pastor thought for a minute. Then he said, "Doug, when you see some plants just coming up in a garden, you don't know, unless someone tells you what kind of plants they are, whether they are going to have beans on them, or tomatoes, or something else. But when they grow up, then they begin to have the right kind of fruit on them. That is the way it is with boys. When boys are not yet grown up, we cannot always tell what God wants them to be. He lets them grow and helps them to decide later on, if they ask Him."

"Oh," said Doug happily, "then I do not need to know now what I am going to be when I grow up."

Then he looked sad again. "But Ed and Jim and Harold have all decided what they are going to be."

"Yes," said the pastor, "they think now that they know. But it may be that God will show them something else by the time they grow older. Ed says he is going to be a pilot. Perhaps God will want him to be a farmer. Then what will you do, Ed?"

"I will be a farmer," said Ed, "and not a pilot. I want to be what God wants me to be."

"Very good," said the pastor. "And I am sure Jim and Harold feel the same way." The two other boys nodded their heads in agreement.

"God makes us all different," the pastor said. "Some boys are stronger than others. Some boys can think better than others. If God has not made you strong, you know that He does not want you to have a job that requires a great deal of strength. That is one way we can tell about the jobs He wants us to have—by the abilities He has given us. Keep thinking about the many ways there are to serve God. Ask Him to show you the right way at the right time, and He will."

"Thank you, Pastor," said the children. "Now we will not worry about what we are going to be when we grow up. We will think about it and pray about it, but not worry about it."

Questions:

1. When does God tell us what He wants us to be?
2. Can you think of some ways He helps us to know?
3. How can you be now what God wants you to be? How can you serve Him now, as a child?

A Scripture verse:

God has given each of us the ability to do certain things well *(Romans 12:6).*

A hymn to sing:

> Take my life, and let it be
> Consecrated, Lord to Thee;
> Take my hands, and let them move
> At the impulse of Thy love,
> At the impulse of Thy love.

29

The Wrong Boy for a Friend

The telephone rang, and Bob went to answer it. "Yes," he said, "this is Bob. All right, I'll go and ask my mother."

"Mother," he said, "Gordon wants me to come over and play. May I play with him this afternoon?"

Mother did not say yes immediately. Instead she looked thoughtful. Finally she said, "Yes, this time you may." And Bob rushed back to the phone to tell Gordon that he would be over right away.

Before he left, Mother said, "Bob, I am not very happy to have you playing too often with Gordon. He does many things that I do not want you ever to do. If you are with him often I am afraid that you will learn to do some of those things too."

"Oh, Mother," Bob said, "Gordon is a very nice boy, and he is my friend. We won't do anything wrong."

When Bob came in, Gordon said, "Why do you always ask your mother if you can come over? Why not just come on over, and if she doesn't like it, well, that's just too bad."

"Oh, no," said Bob, "I must do what Mother tells me to do, otherwise she would give me a spanking."

"I have never had a spanking in all my life that I can remember," Gordon boasted. "My mother doesn't believe in it."

"My mother does," said Bob. "She told me the Bible says that when I do bad things a spanking is good for me. She says that if she doesn't spank me when I'm bad, then I may grow up wrong."

"You won't grow up to be bad," said Gordon. "Look at me. I'm not so bad, and I never get spanked. Well, come on, let's go over to old lady Dinsmore's and try to catch her cat. We can put the cat in a sack and then go down to the river and drown it and put it back on her porch. Boy, will she be surprised!"

"I don't think we ought to drown her cat," Bob said.

"Don't be a sissy," said Gordon. "I suppose your mother wouldn't like it?"

"No, she wouldn't like it at all," said Bob.

"Well, just forget about your mother and come on. We're going to have fun," said Gordon.

So Bob went along.

The boys tried and tried to catch Mrs. Dinsmore's cat, but it kept getting away from them. It ran out into Mrs. Dinsmore's garden, and the boys ran all through the garden trampling down the tomato plants. Finally Gordon became angry about the cat and picked up a big rock and threw it at a basement window. Then both boys ran as fast as they could so that Mrs. Dinsmore, who was in the front of the house, wouldn't be able to see who had done it.

Later that night when Bob got home, Mother said, "Well, Bob, did you have a nice time?" She didn't sound very happy.

"Yes," said Bob, "we had a very nice time, thank you."

"Bob," said his mother, "Mrs. Dinsmore just telephoned."

Bob stopped still. He was afraid that Mrs. Dinsmore had seen them. His mother continued, "She says you tramped down her tomato plants and broke a window in her basement. Did you?"

"Yes," said Bob, "we did."

"Why did you do it?" Mother wanted to know.

"I didn't want to do it," Bob said, "but Gordon wanted to, and he called me a sissy and said I ought to come and help him even when I knew that you didn't want me to."

"Did God want you to?" asked his mother.

"Oh, no!" said Bob. "God did not want me to do it at all."

"Bob," said his mother, "probably I shouldn't have let you go over to Gordon's. It's not good for boys who want to obey God to spend so much time with boys who don't want to do what God says. It's not good to be friends with people like that. And now," she said, "I am sorry that I am going to have to spank you for what you have done."

So Mother gave Bob a spanking right there in the kitchen. Bob cried because the spanking hurt. But afterward he said, "Mother, I'm sorry that I did such a bad thing. Now I think I'll go upstairs and ask God to forgive me."

Questions:

1. Why didn't Bob's mother want him to play with Gordon?
2. What did the boys do?
3. What did Bob's mother do?
4. Why did Bob go upstairs afterward?

A Scripture verse:

Oh, the joys of those who do not follow evil men's advice *(Psalm 1:1)*.

A hymn to sing:

> Take time to be holy,
> Speak oft with thy Lord;
> Abide in Him always,
> And feed on His Word.
> Make friends of God's children;
> Help those who are weak;
> Forgetting in nothing
> His blessing to seek.

30

When Becky Didn't Obey Her Mother

Becky and Peggy lived in two houses that were side by side. The two girls had fun playing together, and they did most everything together. But there was one thing that was different about them. Peggy always did the things her mother asked, but Becky didn't like to obey her parents. That is, until the day that I am going to tell you about.

On this particular day, Becky's mother told her that she was going to the store for a few minutes with Peggy's mother. "I'd like you to pick some berries in our backyard," Becky's mother said. "Perhaps Peggy will help you. Don't pick any in the yard across the street where the old empty house is."

As soon as both their mothers had gone to the store, Becky and Peggy took some pans and went into the backyard to pick berries. Pretty soon Becky said, "I don't think these berries are very thick. I think they are thicker across the street. I am going over there to pick."

"Oh, no," said Peggy, "your mother told you not to."

"Oh, I don't care," said Becky. "Come on, let's go."

"No," said Peggy. "I mind my mother, and my mother wouldn't want me to go over there with you if your mother doesn't want you to go."

"Oh, come on!" said Becky. "My mother won't care."

"I'm not going to," said Peggy. "I'm going to obey my mother. Our mothers know what is best for us."

Peggy kept picking the berries in Becky's backyard, but Becky went across the street to pick. Before long she came back. Her pan was full of berries while Peggy's pan was only half full. "See," said Becky, "the berries were twice as big over there as they are here. You should have come along."

"No," said Peggy, "I shouldn't. I'm glad I stayed here."

"My mother is going to give your mother all the berries you pick," Becky told Peggy. "Come on over, and I'll show you where the thickest patch is."

"No," said Peggy. "My mother would rather have me obey than have a lot of berries."

After a while their mothers came from the store. When Peggy's mother saw how many berries Becky had she said, "Why, Becky, you certainly are a fast picker! Peggy, you are very slow."

But when Becky's mother looked at the berries she said, "Becky, did you go across the street?"

"No," said Becky, "I didn't."

"These look like berries from across the street. They don't look like our berries," said Becky's mother.

The next morning Becky's mother said that Becky couldn't go out to play. She was sick. Becky had red itchy bumps all over her body. "There was poison ivy all over among the berries in the yard across the street," said Becky's mother. "That is why I didn't want her to go over there to pick berries. She disobeyed me, and now she is sick."

When we disobey our mothers and fathers it does not mean that we will always get sick. But it does always mean that the Lord Jesus is sorry that we have not been obedient. Always remember that Jesus wants obedient children.

Questions:

1. What does it mean to disobey?
2. How did Becky disobey her mother?
3. What happened to her?
4. If we disobey our mothers and fathers, will we always get poison ivy?

A Scripture verse:

You children must always obey your fathers and mothers, for that pleases the Lord *(Colossians 3:20).*

A hymn to sing:

> More love to Thee, O Christ,
> More love to Thee!
> Hear Thou the prayer I make
> On bended knee;
> This is my earnest plea;
> More love, O Christ, to Thee,
> More love to Thee,
> More love to Thee!

31

The Popularity Contest

Cindy was as happy as a lark when she came home from school one day.

"Oh, Mother," she said, "we're going to have the most fun tomorrow. We girls decided to have a popularity contest, and each of us is going to tell which one we like best. I hope everybody will say they like me best, don't you, Mother?"

"Well," said Mother, "I don't know about that. I remember once when I was a little girl about your age—"

Cindy's eyes began to shine because she knew Mother was going to tell her a story. Mother always told the best stories.

"Oh, Mother," she said, "tell me the story."

"Well," said Mother, "when I was a little girl we had a contest once, and I felt just about the way you do. I wanted to win the contest badly. We girls in the fourth grade had decided to vote on which of us was the nicest in the room. I thought I was the nicest because I had such pretty hair and because I laughed a lot and liked to play. There was another girl named Sally that we all liked too. Sally wasn't as noisy, and she always was best in spelling tests, and she was good in arithmetic, too.

"We held the contest one day after school. And do you know who won? Nobody did. Sally got half the notes and I got half. There were twelve of us in the room. Six had voted for Sally, and six had voted for me, so we decided to vote again. Just before we voted, I saw Sally whispering to one of the girls who had voted for her before. And do you know what? The girl voted for me the next time instead of for Sally. Sally had asked her to vote for me instead. So I won the contest.

"Afterward, I thought maybe Sally wouldn't want to walk home from school with me as she usually did, because I had won and she hadn't. But she didn't seem any different. 'I'm so glad you won,' Sally told me. And I said, 'But I won only because you asked Barbara to vote for me instead of you the second time.'

" 'Well,' said Sally, 'that was all right because I think you should have won. After all, I like you better than I like me.'

"How ashamed I was of myself, because I liked myself better than I liked Sally! From that time on I began to try to think how nice other people were, instead of how nice I was!

"Sally helped me a lot, and she became one of my very best friends. In fact, it was Sally who asked me to go to Sunday school with her and asked the teacher to tell me about Jesus. So you see I owe a lot to Sally. But if I had won the contest and hadn't known that Sally helped me, I might have been very proud and stuck up. I might not have wanted to go to Sunday school with Sally after that."

Cindy was quiet for a little while. Then she said, "Mother, I don't think I want to win the contest tomorrow. I don't think it would be good for me. I want to be like Sally and help someone else win it. I want to help people love Jesus, not just try to have them like me."

Questions:

1. Why did Sally ask Barbara to vote for Cindy's mother?
2. What important thing happened to Cindy's mother because Sally made her win?
3. If Sally had been proud and wanted to win the contest, what might have happened?

A Scripture verse:

Charm can be deceptive and beauty doesn't last, but a woman who fears and reverences God shall be greatly praised *(Proverbs 31:30)*.

A hymn to sing:

> I'm a child of the King,
> A child of the King:
> With Jesus my Saviour,
> I'm a child of the King.

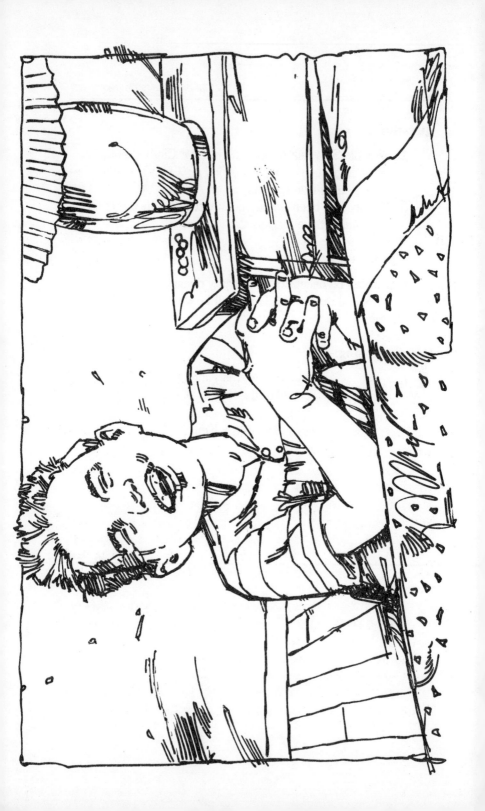

32

Peter's Prayer

Peter was only five years old and he couldn't read yet, but he kept holding the letter in front of him and looking at it just as though he could. Of course he wasn't really reading it, but he was thinking about it. In fact he was thinking about it a lot. He knew what the letter said, because Daddy had just read it to him.

The letter was from Uncle Doug, who was a missionary doctor out in Africa. It told about a little girl twelve years old who had come to live with Uncle Doug and Aunt Betty. This little girl had never been in a house before, so Uncle Doug had to show her how to turn the knob and open the front door. The little girl wasn't a Christian yet either, and in his letter Uncle Doug had asked people to pray for her so that she would come to know the Lord Jesus.

Uncle Doug's letter said that just the Sunday before, twenty-nine people had decided to accept Jesus as Savior. These people had heard about Jesus because they were sick and had come to the hospital. There the doctors and nurses told them how much Jesus loved them.

But Peter kept thinking most of all about something else that Uncle Doug had said. He kept thinking about the part of the letter that said that if people prayed for these twenty-nine new Christians they would "grow in the Lord." Peter knew what Uncle Doug meant. He meant that they might be better Christians a year from now if people would pray for them. Uncle Doug had also said that if people didn't pray for them, in another year some of them might not love the Lord Jesus anymore or might not work for Him anymore.

Peter decided that the only thing for him to do was to pray for those twenty-nine people so that they would become strong Christians. That night he got down on his knees beside his bed just before getting in and said, "Lord Jesus, please help those twenty-nine people become strong Christians. And please help the little girl who didn't know how to open the door to become a Christian."

Peter prayed about them every night for a long time.

Meanwhile out in Africa the little girl who was staying at Uncle Doug's began to hear about the Lord Jesus. She didn't know very much about Him, just as she didn't know very much about houses. But now she began to hear that the Lord Jesus had died for her sins and that if she asked the Lord Jesus to forgive her, He would.

In a few days she decided that she would really like the Lord Jesus to come into her heart, and she told Uncle Doug about it. Uncle Doug was very glad and helped her to understand more about all that Jesus had done for her. Then she said, "Thank You, Lord Jesus, for forgiving my sins, and help me to be a good girl." Of course she said it in another language and not in words that you or I could understand.

That night Uncle Doug told Aunt Betty about it, and he said, "I think people must have been praying for her. I am glad that I asked people to pray when I wrote the letter."

Do you know who had been praying for her?

Questions:

1. Why were the twenty-nine people at the hospital?
2. Did God hear Peter's prayer? Does He hear your prayers?
3. When and where did Peter pray for the little girl?

A Scripture verse:

Always keep on praying *(1 Thessalonians 5:17)*.

A hymn to sing:

> Sweet hour of prayer, sweet hour of prayer,
> That calls me from a world of care,
> And bids me at my Father's throne
> Make all my wants and wishes known.

33

The Picnic

Debbie and John were cousins. They lived just a few houses away from each other and played together a lot.

One day Debbie's parents and John's parents decided both families should go on a picnic beside a lake several miles away. Both children woke up early the day of the picnic.

Debbie looked out the window of her room and saw the sun shining and heard the birds singing, and she thought, *What a wonderful day for our picnic. I'll telephone John and see if he is awake yet.* Just as she reached for the telephone, it started ringing. Who do you suppose was calling? It was John!

After they had talked for a while, Mother told Debbie breakfast was ready. Debbie told John she had to go.

"OK," John said. "Daddy says to be ready at nine, and both cars can travel along together."

"All right," Debbie said, "we'll see you soon."

Debbie was so excited about the picnic that she thought nine o'clock would never come. But, sure enough, it did! Soon both families were driving down the highway, headed toward the lake.

John's family was ahead, but soon they pulled off the highway to a gas station. So Debbie's father stopped at the gas station too.

John's father came over. "Guess what!" he said. "I've got a flat tire!"

So the children played while the tire was being changed.

"Why don't you come with us in our car?" John asked.

"I already asked, but Daddy said, 'No, not this time,'" Debbie told him. "But you know what? I don't care. I'm going to anyway. He wouldn't spank me or anything at a picnic."

"All aboard," John's father finally called.

Everyone got back into the cars, and John's family started off.

But Debbie wasn't in the car with her family.

"Where's Debbie?" her older sister asked.

"She said she was going in the other car the rest of the way," her little brother said.

Debbie's father was angry, but there was nothing to do but start the car. It was a beautiful morning and everyone had a fairly nice time riding along, except that they were sorry about what Debbie had done. After about an hour they arrived at the lake.

Debbie's father went to the other car, but he didn't see Debbie there. "Where's Debbie?" he exclaimed to John's father. "Wasn't she with you?"

"No," John's father answered. "She must still be back at the gas station!"

"Oh, no!" Debbie's mother said, and she began to cry.

Debbie's father got into his car and hurried back. Sure enough, there she was with the gas station man. She had been crying, but the nice gas station man told her not to worry, because her family would soon notice she was missing and come back.

"Debbie, where were you?" her daddy exclaimed, hugging her with relief that she was found.

"I was in the bathroom," Debbie explained, "and when I came out, you were gone."

Debbie's father thanked the gas station man for taking care of her, and they started back to the lake. "Your brother said you had gone in the other car," Debbie's father said.

Debbie looked ashamed. "Yes, you told me I couldn't, but I was going to anyway."

"You planned to disobey me," he said, "and I must punish you." So he stopped the car and spanked her there beside the road.

After Debbie stopped crying, she told her father, "I'm sorry, Daddy. Look at all the trouble I caused by disobeying you."

"I'm glad you realize it," her father said, "and I hope you won't disobey again. But if you do, I'll love you just as much—and I'll spank you again. God gave you to me, and He wants me to teach you to do what is right. Sometimes He too has to punish His children. He loves us and wants us to learn to do what is best."

"I'm glad God made me your little girl, Daddy," said Debbie, "and I love you too."

Questions:

1. What did Debbie plan to do that was bad?
2. What did her father do to her? Why? Give two reasons.
3. Why does God punish His children sometimes?

A Scripture verse:

Don't be angry when the Lord punishes you. . . . For when He punishes you, it proves that He loves you. When He whips you it proves you are really His child *(Hebrews 12:5-6)*.

A hymn to sing:

> I'm a child of the King,
> A child of the King:
> With Jesus my Saviour,
> I'm a child of the King.

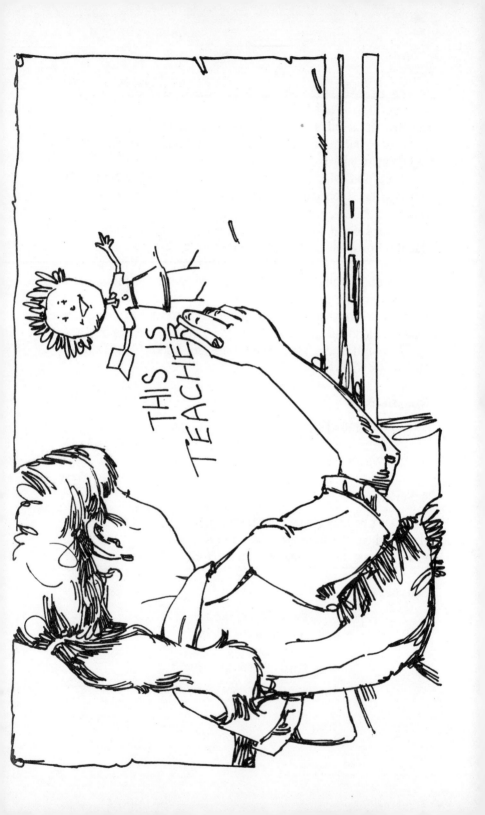

34

Debbie Prays for an Enemy

Everyone said that Alice Brown was a mean little girl. She often did bad things. She liked to make fun of the other children and get them into trouble.

But when Alice was in school she behaved, and the teacher thought that Alice was a nice little girl.

One day during recess Alice went into her room at school and drew a funny face on the board and wrote under it, "This is Teacher." Then she ran outside again to play.

There was a girl in the same room with Alice whose name was Debbie. Debbie was kind to everyone, and maybe that is the reason Alice didn't like her. Alice wished that she could be kind, and, because she wasn't, she was jealous of Debbie and was always trying to make trouble for her.

So that day after recess when all the children came into the room, they were surprised and sorry when they saw that someone had drawn a funny picture on the board and written that it was the teacher. Everyone, that is, except Alice.

Teacher stopped for a special lesson when she came in. She said, "Children, it is wrong to make fun of other people and that includes the teacher, doesn't it? I wonder who drew the picture?"

Alice put up her hand.

"Alice," asked the teacher, "did you put the picture on the board?

"No," said Alice, "I didn't draw it, but I know who did."

"Well, then," said the teacher, "who was it?"

"It was Debbie," said Alice.

Debbie was very surprised, and her face got red.

"Yes," said the teacher, "I can see that Debbie was the one. Debbie, I am sorry that you have done this. You must stay after school."

The other children knew that Debbie had not drawn the picture on the board. They all thought Alice had done it, and they were very angry with her.

That afternoon when school was out, Debbie had to stay for twenty minutes before she could go home. When the teacher finally told her she could go, she went out and was getting ready to ride her bicycle home.

Several of the other children were there and so was Alice. Alice was very angry because her bicycle had a flat tire. She remembered riding through some pieces of broken glass on the way to school that morning, and now she found a piece of glass in the tire.

Alice was not only angry, but she was worried because she had a paper route. If she didn't get the papers to the people on time, they might not want to keep taking the paper from her.

When Debbie saw what had happened, she was very glad at first. The other children were too, and they were laughing and making fun of Alice. Debbie thought, *It serves her right for telling a lie about me.*

Do you know that it is wrong for Christian boys and girls to be angry? The Lord is in the hearts of those who love Him, and He tells them, just as the Bible says, to love their enemies instead of trying to get even with them.

The Lord Jesus tells them to return good for evil, and He tells people to help others even when the people do mean, bad things to them.

That is why Debbie could not stay angry very long. She began to think, *Poor Alice. I am sorry that she isn't going to be able to deliver her papers on time.*

And then before she quite knew what she was saying, Debbie said, "Alice, why don't you use my bicycle tonight? But be careful with it, and bring it back when you are through with it."

Alice and the other children were very, very surprised.

Alice was so ashamed of herself for what she had done to Debbie. She felt a little better next day, after she had told the whole story to the teacher and apologized.

You will not be surprised to know it was not long afterwards that Alice began going to a Bible club with Debbie. There she learned about the Lord Jesus, and Alice and Debbie became good friends.

Questions:

1. If Debbie had just laughed at Alice because her bike had a flat tire, would Alice have wanted to hear about Jesus?
2. Why was Alice ashamed of herself?
3. When you treat someone kindly after he has been unkind to you, how will he feel?

A Scripture verse:

If your enemy is hungry, give him food! If he is thirsty, give him something to drink! This will make him feel ashamed of himself, and God will reward you *(Proverbs 25:21-22)*.

A hymn to sing:

He leadeth me, He leadeth me!
By His own hand He leadeth me!
His faithful follower I would be,
For by His hand He leadeth me.

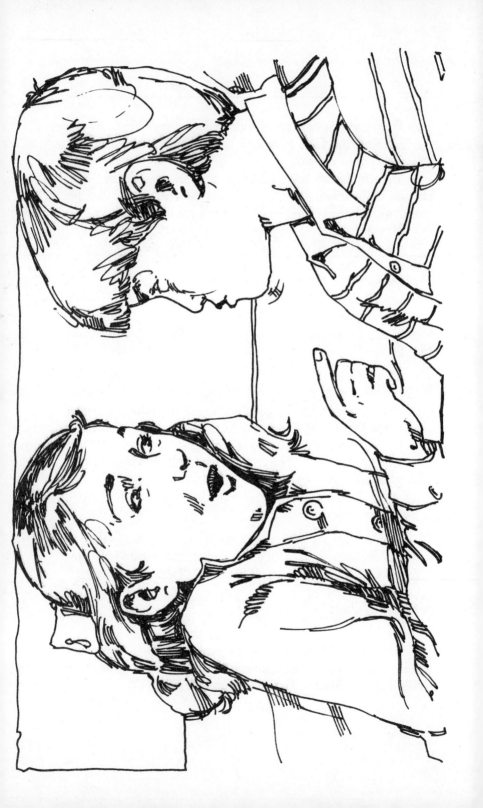

35

A Quarrel and How It Was Ended

It was a dark, rainy day with the wind blowing hard in the trees. Peggy Jo and Karen and Tim played all the different inside games they could think of, but finally they just couldn't think of anything else to do.

"Mother," said Karen, "would you tell us a story about when you were a little girl?"

"Oh, yes," said Peggy Jo, "that would be such fun."

"Yes," said Tim. "I like to hear Mother's stories."

"Well," said Mother, "I suppose I could. I can tell it to you while I am mending."

"Goody!" shouted the children as they gathered around Mother.

"Shall I tell you the story about the time there was a quarrel?" Mother asked.

"I don't like to hear about quarreling and fighting," said Peggy Jo.

"No," said Mother, "it is not very pleasant, is it? But sometimes there are quarrels even around here, and maybe this story would help you children to stop quarreling."

"All right," said Peggy Jo. "Will you please tell us the story?"

"Well," said Mother, "there was a little girl on our street who wasn't very nice. We'll call her Barbara. She was always calling the other children names, and so of course the other children didn't like her very well. And some of the other children called her names too.

"Barbara said she was a Christian, but she certainly didn't act like one.

"There was a boy whom she especially liked to tease. We'll call him Mark. He had red hair, so she teased him about the color of his hair. Barbara called him 'Red' and said he ought to be a fireman because his hair was on fire. That made Mark very angry, so he called Barbara some names too, although I don't remember just what they were now.

"Mark was a Christian, and he loved the Lord Jesus, but he hadn't yet learned how to be kind to other people when they were not kind to him.

"The quarrel between this boy and girl grew worse, and it must have hurt the Lord Jesus very much to see His children acting that way.

"Three other children were walking home from school one day and talking about the quarrel between Mark and Barbara. The three children loved the Lord Jesus, and they knew Jesus was unhappy about the quarrel.

" 'What can we do,' they asked themselves, 'to help them to be friends?'

"One of the three children had a good idea. He said, 'Let's all pray tonight for Barbara and Mark. And let's pray for them every night, just before we go to bed, for a whole week.'

"So that is just what the three children did. They prayed every night for a whole week for the little boy and girl to stop quarreling.

"And do you know what happened? About three days later, Mark was walking home from school, and Barbara was a little way behind him. She was just getting ready to yell, 'Red is a fireman, Red is a fireman,' when she thought about something. She thought about a verse she had learned that week in Sunday school that said to be kind to other people. I guess the Lord was answering the prayers of the three children. The Holy Spirit was talking to the little girl and telling her to be kind instead of calling the little boy names.

"Barbara already had her mouth wide open ready to yell at Mark, when she suddenly closed it and ran to catch up with him.

"But as soon as he saw her coming, he began to call her a sour apple and other things and started to run away.

" 'Mark,' called Barbara, 'please don't run away. I want to tell you something.' He stopped in surprise as she caught up with him. She said, 'I'm sorry that I called you Red the fireman.'

"Mark was so surprised that he didn't know what to do. 'Well then,' he said, 'I'm sorry I called you a sour apple, and we can be friends from now on.'

And sure enough, that is just what happened.

Questions:

1. How did the quarrel start?
2. If the little boy had just laughed when the little girl teased him, would there have been a quarrel?
3. What did the three children decide to do about it?
4. Who helped the little girl change her mind?

A Scripture verse:

Happy are those who strive for peace—they shall be called the sons of God *(Matthew 5:9).*

A hymn to sing:

> Take the name of Jesus with you,
> Child of sorrow and of woe;
> It will joy and comfort give you,
> Take it, then, where'er you go.

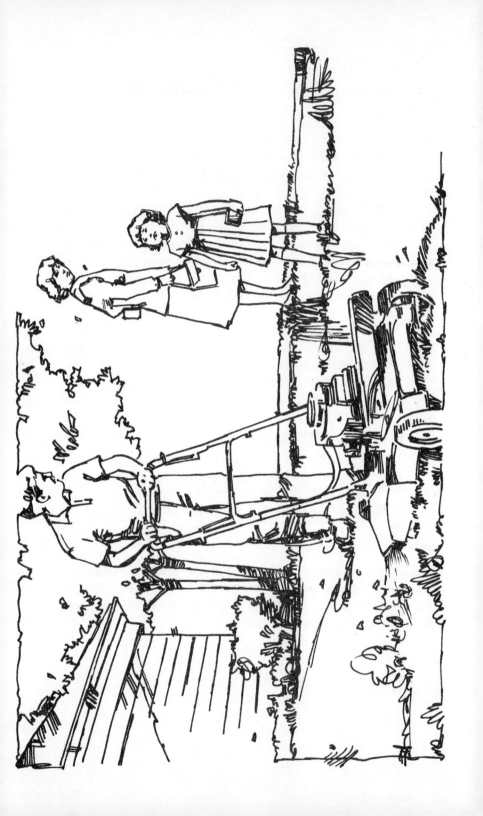

36

The Story of Jane's Father

Jane's father laughed when she asked him to go to church with her.

"Why should I want to go to church?" he asked. "I'm not a Christian, you know. You and Mother go as much as you want to, but you had better let me stay home and do the lawn. It's going to begin looking like a hayfield around here!"

"But, Daddy," Jane said, "it's important to go to church. It's important to know about God and what He wants us to do."

"But I don't think I believe in God," Jane's father said. "Why does He let so many people get sick and get hurt? And anyway, I'm too busy to think about God. I have to think about my work."

So Jane and Mother went to church, and Daddy stayed home to mow the lawn and read the paper. Jane was very sad. Just last night she had prayed again, asking God to make her daddy love Jesus too, just as Jane and her mother did.

"I know God is going to answer my prayer about Daddy," Jane told her mother, "but I wish that it would be soon."

"Perhaps it will be," her mother said. "We'll just keep praying."

While Jane and her mother were at church, Daddy read the paper for quite a while and then went out to mow the lawn. But Daddy didn't seem to be enjoying Sunday at home as he usually did. He kept thinking about what Jane had said. He said to himself, "I wish I were as kind and nice as my little girl is and as my wife is. They go to church and believe in Jesus and God, and they are kind and nice. I wonder, if I went to church, if it wouldn't help me to be kind, as I want to be."

Daddy kept mowing the lawn. He liked to mow lawns. But this morning it didn't seem very much fun to mow the lawn. He couldn't think of anything that would be very much fun. Finally he left the lawn mower out on the lawn and went into the house and looked around through the bookcase until he found a Bible.

"Jane and her mother read this Book an awful lot," he said, "and I used to read it when I was a boy. I remember there was a verse I learned once in the book of John. I think it was in the third chapter. It was about God loving me and sending Jesus to die for me. I wish I could find it."

Jane's father finally found the book of John and the third chapter and began reading it. Finally he came to the sixteenth verse, and this is what he read: "For God so loved the world, that he gave his only begotten Son, that whosoever believeth on him should not perish but have everlasting life."

"Good," said Jane's father, "that's it. That's the verse I used to know." He read the verse several times, and then he went out to mow the lawn again. He kept thinking and thinking about that verse. "God loves me," he said to himself. "Jesus died for me." And then he remembered, "But I don't believe in God, so I don't believe that verse." Then he began to mow the lawn as fast as he could and tried to forget what he had read in the Bible.

The next morning while Jane's father was driving to work, he couldn't forget the verse he had read Sunday morning. "Just think," he said to himself, "Jesus died for me! God loves me!" Then all of a sudden he slowed down the car and brought it to a stop at the side of the road. He bowed his head and said, "God, thank You for sending Jesus to die for me. I believe in You, and I want You to save me. Thank You for saving me."

Daddy seemed very happy when he got home from work that night, but he didn't tell Mother and Jane what had happened. In fact, he kept the secret for a whole week. But the next Sunday morning when Jane said, "Daddy, I wish you would go to church with us this morning," he said, "Why, sure, I've been planning on it." Jane was so surprised she hardly knew what to think. Then Daddy told Jane and Mother what had happened, and of course they were very happy.

Before they started to church, Jane went up to her room and knelt down beside her bed and said, "Thank You, God! Oh, thank You for helping our whole family to love You."

Questions:

1. Did Jane's father believe in God at first?
2. What did Jane do?
3. Tell about how Jane's father found the Bible verse, and what he thought about it.
4. When did Jane's father tell Jane and her mother that he had become a Christian?

A Scripture verse:

For whatever God says to us is full of living power: It is sharper than the sharpest dagger, cutting swift and deep into our innermost thoughts and desires with all their parts, exposing us for what we really are *(Hebrews 4:12)*.

A hymn to sing:

> Just now, your doubtings give o'er;
> Just now, reject Him no more;
> Just now, throw open the door;
> Let Jesus come into your heart.

37

The Stolen Bicycle

Priscilla couldn't find her bike. It wasn't in the garage where it was supposed to be, and it wasn't in the yard. It wasn't anywhere.

"I don't think you put it away last night," said Bill, Priscilla's big brother. "The last time I saw it, it was sitting on the sidewalk. If you forgot to put it away, maybe someone came when it was dark and stole it."

Priscilla thought that was probably what had happened, and she started to cry. The bicycle was gone. It was a good bicycle, and she used it a lot. It was a lot of fun, and now it was gone.

"I think I know who stole it," Priscilla said.

Bill looked surprised. "How could you ever know that?" he asked.

"Just because," said Priscilla. "It was Donald. He likes my bike. Just the other day he asked me if he could ride it, and I told him no."

"Don't be foolish," said her brother. "You don't know that he took it, so don't tell anybody that he did."

"He did, though," said Priscilla. "I'm sure he did." And she went next door to tell the children there that Donald had stolen her bike. Pretty soon the whole neighborhood had heard that Donald had stolen Priscilla's bicycle.

Donald was surprised when the children said he was a bad boy for stealing the bicycle. "I didn't steal it," he said.

"Oh, yes, you did," they all said. "Priscilla said you did, and Priscilla knows."

"Honest, I didn't!" said Donald. "You can come and see."

But all the children kept calling Donald a bad boy and wouldn't play with him, so he had to go home.

When he went to school that afternoon, all the children pointed at him and yelled, "Thief! Robber!" and some of the girls started singing over and over again,

> "Donald is a robber,
> Donald is a robber!"

That afternoon after school Priscilla and some of her friends decided to play house. The house was going to be in some bushes at the side of the yard. They ran to the bushes, and all of a sudden Priscilla shouted, "Look! Look! My bicycle!" and gave a squeal of delight.

Sure enough, there was her bicycle, hidden in the tall grass. "Now I remember," she said. "I left it here last night when Mother called me to supper, and I forgot to put it away. Oh, goody, goody! I have my bicycle again."

"Goody, goody!" the other children said too. "Priscilla has her bicycle again!"

Poor Donald! Even when Priscilla told the children that she had forgotten where she left the bike, the children could only remember that they had called Donald a thief. "He probably stole the bicycle and then put it back there in the bushes," they decided.

"Donald," Priscilla said later, "I'm sorry that I called you a thief. Would you like to go to Sunday school with us tomorrow?"

"No," said Donald, "I haven't ever been to Sunday school, and I don't want to go to your Sunday school. I don't think it is a very good Sunday school, because they teach you to call a person a thief when he hasn't stolen anything. I don't want to go to your Sunday school."

And he didn't, even though Priscilla asked him many times.

Priscilla was very sorry for what she had done. She learned a lesson. She decided that never again was she going to think or say that somebody had done something unless she was absolutely sure.

She asked God to forgive her.

Questions:

1. Did Priscilla see Donald take her bicycle?
2. Did anyone see Donald take Priscilla's bike?
3. Why did Priscilla think he had taken it?
4. What happened to Donald?

A Scripture verse:

Don't extort money by threats and violence; don't accuse anyone of what you know he didn't do; and be content with your pay *(Luke 3:14)*.

A hymn to sing:

> Yield not to temptation,
> For yielding is sin,
> Each victory will help you
> Some other to win;
> Fight manfully onward,
> Dark passions subdue,
> Look ever to Jesus,
> He will carry you through.

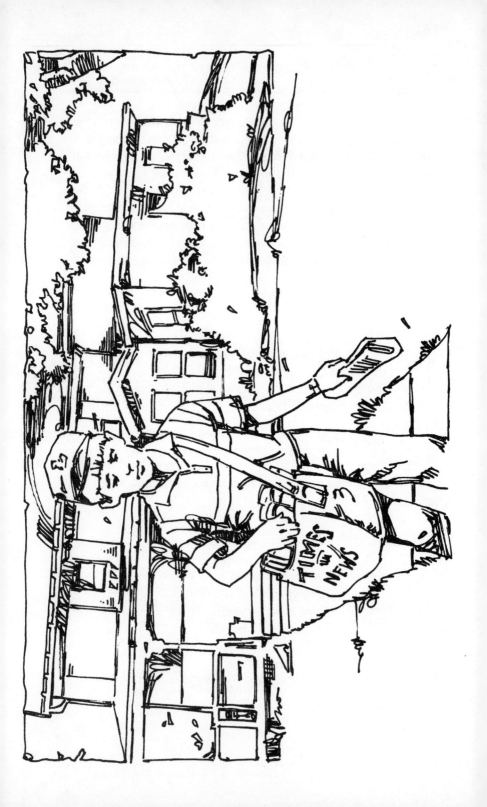

38

Some Money for God's House

Dick had a paper route after school, but he didn't have a bicycle. It took a long, long time to walk from house to house with his papers.

They were heavy, too, and sometimes they hurt his shoulder during the first part of the walk until he had delivered enough so that his newspaper sack was lighter. And by that time his feet were tired, so it didn't help very much, even if he had fewer papers left.

"What I need," Dick kept telling himself, "is a bicycle. I want a nice red bicycle with a wire rack in front of it to carry my papers in."

One day Dick told his mother how much he needed a bicycle.

She said, "Well, why don't you buy one? You earn about four dollars a week on your paper route. How much would a good used bicycle cost?"

Dick didn't know, but he decided to find out. He went down to see Mr. Jackson at the bicycle shop.

"Mr. Jackson," he said, "do you have a good used bicycle that I could buy?"

"Yes," said Mr. Jackson, "I have a very good one here that I have just taken apart and fixed and put back together again. Would you like to see it?"

"How much does it cost?" Dick asked.

"It costs sixteen dollars," Mr. Jackson said. "It's a very good buy." Mr. Jackson brought the bicycle out for Dick to see.

"Oh, boy!" he said. "What a beautiful bicycle! And it is red, and it has a wire rack in front of it. It is just what I need. I am going to try to earn enough money to buy it."

Dick ran home to tell his mother.

Dick had had his paper route for two weeks, and he already had eight dollars in the bank. In two more weeks he would have sixteen dollars, and then he could buy the bicycle.

Every day Dick went down to see the beautiful red bicycle. He thought it was the best bicycle he had ever seen. Soon it would be his very own.

One week went by, and then Dick had twelve dollars. Finally Dick had the sixteen dollars. He took his money and hurried to the bicycle shop to see Mr. Jackson.

Another boy was there looking at the bicycle.

"That is a very good bicycle," the other boy said. "I want to buy it. I will go home and get the money."

"No," said Mr. Jackson, "Dick is here with his money, and he is going to buy it. If Dick has sixteen dollars, he can have the bicycle. Do you have sixteen dollars, Dick?"

"Yes," said Dick happily, "and now I can buy the bicycle."

Just then Dick thought of something. As soon as he began to think about it, he tried to think of something else. He tried to pretend that he hadn't thought about it at all. But no matter how hard he tried, he kept right on thinking about it anyway, and it became a bigger and a bigger thought. Finally Dick had to think about it.

This was the thought: Dick had forgotten to give part of the sixteen dollars to the Lord Jesus. Dick always gave part of the money he earned to the Lord. Sometimes he gave a tenth, and sometimes he gave more. Sometimes he gave all that he earned.

How much is one-tenth of sixteen dollars? Dick wondered. He didn't know, so he asked Mr. Jackson. "Mr. Jackson, how much is one-tenth of sixteen dollars?"

"That would be a dollar and sixty cents," Mr. Jackson said.

"Oh," said Dick.

Dick thought about the bicycle and how much he needed it. He thought about the other boy who was going to buy the bicycle if he didn't. He wondered if the Lord would mind if just this once he spent all the money instead of giving his tithe.

But if I did, Dick said to himself, *then probably I would do it again some other time. Then I might keep on doing it and pretty soon I wouldn't be giving money to the Lord as I want to.*

Dick blinked back the tears. "I don't think I'll buy the bicycle," he said to Mr. Jackson.

"Won't buy the bicycle?" Mr. Jackson was very much surprised. "Why, I thought this bicycle was just the one you wanted."

"It is," said Dick, "but I don't have enough money."

"Yes, you do, Dick," said Mr. Jackson, looking at the money in Dick's hand. "You have sixteen dollars, and that is just what you need."

"No, all of this sixteen dollars isn't mine," Dick said. "A dollar and sixty cents of it belongs to the Lord."

Mr. Jackson looked surprised. Then Mr. Jackson looked embarrassed. His face got red. Mr. Jackson remembered that he had not given any of his money to the Lord for a very long time. Mr. Jackson had told people that he loved the Lord Jesus, and he thought now that he hadn't been showing it very well. God was teaching him a lesson through Dick.

"Well," he said, "I think you are doing the right thing in not buying the bicycle. I think you should give the dollar sixty cents to the Lord. I guess I must sell the bicycle to this other boy as I said I would."

The other boy ran home to get his money.

Dick started to leave.

"Just a minute," Mr. Jackson said. "I want to show you something, Dick. Here is another bicycle that I have now. It is a better bicycle than the one you were going to buy."

"How much does it cost?" Dick wanted to know.

"Let's see," said Mr. Jackson, "that would be fourteen dollars and forty cents. Yes, that's what it costs, Dick, fourteen dollars and forty cents."

"I wonder if I have that much," Dick said. "How much will I have left when I take a dollar sixty out of the sixteen dollars I have?"

"Well, bless me," said Mr. Jackson, "you'll have just fourteen dollars and forty cents—just the amount you need."

Both Dick and Mr. Jackson were very happy. Dick gave Mr. Jackson fourteen dollars and forty cents and rode off on his bicycle.

Mr. Jackson looked out the door after him. *Lord,* he prayed in his heart, *thank You for teaching me a lesson today through Dick. Help me to always remember the lesson I've learned today.*

Questions:

1. Can you guess what the lesson was that Mr. Jackson learned from Dick?
2. If you earned fifty cents and wanted to give one-tenth of it to the Lord, how much would you give?
3. How could you give the money to God?

A Scripture verse:

But remember this, that if you give little you will get little. A farmer who plants just a few seeds will get only a small crop, but if he plants much, he will reap much *(2 Corinthians 9:6)*.

A hymn to sing:

Give of your best to the Master;
Give Him first place in your heart;
Give Him first place in your service,
Consecrate every part.

39

Some Halloween Fun

It was Halloween, and boys and girls were walking around scaring each other with jack-o-lanterns. Some of the mothers and fathers gave the children candy or cookies or other treats.

Jon's jack-o-lantern was so big he had to pull it in his wagon. Everyone said it was the most wonderful jack-o-lantern they had ever seen.

Billy and Jack came over to see Jon's jack-o-lantern. "Boy!" Jack said. "Is that ever a big one! Let's go over to the old house where the witch lives and scare her with your jack-o-lantern."

"That's a neat idea," said Billy. "I'll bet she'll be so scared she won't know what to do."

"Naw," said Jon, "Mrs. Smith isn't a witch. They just say that because she lives in an old house."

"But some kids have seen her with a broom," said Billy.

"She was probably just sweeping her porch," said Jon. "My mother says she's a nice lady and we shouldn't make fun of her."

"She sure gets awful mad when we tease her," said Billy. "That's why I think it would be fun if we would take Jon's jack-o-lantern and put it on her porch. I bet she would be awful mad."

"I think I have a better idea," Jon said. "Jesus loves Mrs. Smith, because He loves everyone. We ought to like Mrs. Smith too, because we love Jesus. Let's do something nice for her."

"But tonight is Halloween," said Billy. "So we couldn't tonight."

"Sure we can," said Jon. "Jesus loves us on Halloween just as much as at any other time, so we ought to love other people on Halloween, too, instead of trying to hurt them."

"What could we do to be nice to her?" asked Billy.

"What I think," said Jack, "is that we can ask our mothers if we can have some food and leave it on her porch."

Both the other boys thought that was a good idea, so they went home and asked their mothers about it. Pretty soon they came back, and each of them had some food, enough to make a nice boxful to put on Jon's wagon.

The boys were rather scared when they finally got to the old house where Mrs. Smith lived. There weren't any other houses near, and the house was all dark. "I'm kind of scared," said Billy.

"So am I," said Jack.

"So am I," said Jon, "but we had better keep going."

Soon the children were on the old rickety porch. They hauled and dragged and lifted until they got the box up to the top of the steps. They tried to be quiet, but they still made a lot of noise.

Just then they heard a noise inside the house, and before they had a chance to jump off the steps and run away, the door opened and Mrs. Smith came out. She was crying.

"Go away, you bad children!" she said. "Go away and don't try to hurt my things anymore. What have you got in this box? Have you been stealing?"

"Oh, no," said Jon. "It's food. We brought it for you because we wanted to play a nice Halloween trick."

"You brought all this for me?" she said. "Oh, how wonderful! I thought children did only naughty tricks on Halloween."

"Oh, no," the boys told her. "Jesus wants us to always do nice things so that people will know that we belong to Him."

Mrs. Smith seemed surprised. "If belonging to Jesus makes boys act like this, then I wish I belonged to Jesus too."

"Oh, you can, Mrs. Smith!" the boys told her. "Jesus wants you to belong to Him."

"Could my mother come over tomorrow and talk to you about Jesus?" Jon asked.

"Yes, I would like that very much," Mrs. Smith said.

Then the boys rushed home to tell Jon's mother.

"Aren't you glad we gave something instead of making up a bad trick?" Jack asked. "Just because of that, Mrs. Smith is going to belong to Jesus."

Questions:

1. Is it all right to do naughty things on Halloween?
2. Why was Mrs. Smith crying?
3. Was she a witch? Why did the boys think so?
4. Why did Mrs. Smith want to become a Christian?

A Scripture verse:

That's why whenever we can we should always be kind to everyone, and especially to our Christian brothers *(Galatians 6:10).*

A hymn to sing:

> Channels only, blessed Master,
> But with all Thy wondrous power
> Flowing through us, Thou canst use us
> Every day and every hour.

40

The New Boy

Edward hated having to go to a new school, but his father had to move almost every year because of his work. That is why one morning Edward found himself starting off to a new school again.

Edward had red hair, and, sure enough, before he had gone very far some children started calling to him. "Hey, Redhead," they said, "where are you going? Where did you get that red hair?"

"I'm going to school," said Edward. "We just moved here. And don't call me a redhead."

"Why not?" said one of the boys. "We like to call people redheads. Redhead! Redhead!" he yelled at Edward.

"Stop saying that, or I'll hit you," said Edward.

"Is that so?" said the other boy. "I'd just like to see you."

By this time they were at the school. "Hey, you kids, break it up," said one of the teachers crossly when he saw the boys arguing.

Edward had a miserable morning. All the children were looking at him, and many of them were saying unkind things about him. They said that he was rude and quarrelsome. *They called me a redhead first before I said anything,* Edward said to himself. *They didn't have any right to call me a redhead.*

Then Edward thought, *Maybe I shouldn't have gotten mad when they called me a redhead.* He remembered a Bible verse that he had learned. "A soft answer turns away wrath." He remembered that his Sunday school teacher had explained to him that it is easy to start a fight, but it is also easy to keep from fighting by being kind when people are rude. *I think I'll try it,* Edward said to himself.

At recess time the boy who had called him a redhead yelled at him again. "Hey, Redhead, where are you going? Why did you come to our school? Why didn't you stay home?"

Instead of answering roughly, Edward turned around, grinned, and said, "Just be glad my hair isn't green or blue!"

The other boy looked surprised. Edward not angry? He laughed. "That would be funny if your hair was green or blue," he said. "I guess red isn't such a bad color after all."

"Not when you get used to it," Edward said.

"Say," said the other boy, "would you like to play baseball with us?"

"Sure," said Edward.

"Well, then, come along, let's get started," said the other boy.

And they went off together, and soon after that they became good friends.

Edward always remembered the Bible verse because it worked so well.

Questions:

1. What probably would have happened at recess if Edward had given an angry reply?
2. What would have happened in heaven? Who would have been sorry there?
3. Is it easy to have friends when you act in a kind way? How can you easily have enemies?

A Scripture verse:

A soft answer turns away wrath, but harsh words cause quarrels *(Proverbs 15:1)*.

A hymn to sing:

> Take the name of Jesus with you,
> Child of sorrow and of woe;
> It will joy and comfort give you,
> Take it, then, where'er you go.

41

A Letter for Elaine

After the mailman rang the doorbell to show that he had left some letters, Mother went out to get them. Soon she called, "Elaine, here's a letter for you."

"For me?" asked Elaine. "Oh, goody! Who would be writing a letter to me?"

Elaine quickly opened her letter and found that it was from her cousin Elizabeth. In the nice long letter Elizabeth told Elaine about the summer camp where she was. She and many other children were at a pretty place where there were little houses to sleep in and a great big tent where they ate their meals. Elizabeth was learning to swim and was having lots of fun.

"I am to be here for a whole week," Elizabeth wrote. "And it doesn't cost me anything. Everyone in our Sunday school who learned five hundred Bible verses got a week at camp free."

When Elaine finished reading Elizabeth's letter, her eyes were shining. "Oh, if only our Sunday school had a camp where we could go for a week if we learned five hundred verses!" Elaine told her mother. "I'd learn five hundred verses in a hurry."

"That is very nice that the children can do that," said her mother. "But I think more wonderful things will happen to them than going to camp when they learn five hundred verses."

"Oh, Mother," said Elaine, "how could there be?"

"Well," said Mother, "I have learned many verses. I've never been to camp, but I'm glad I learned the verses anyway, because when I need to know what God wants me to do, He tells me through a verse."

"How can He do that?" Elaine wanted to know.

"Oh, that's easy," said Mother. "If I feel cross and cranky, a verse I learned jumps into my mind and says, 'Let the peace of God rule in your hearts.' Then when I start thinking about Jesus and how kind and patient He is, it makes me kind and patient. So I am very glad that I learned that Bible verse a long time ago."

Elaine thought about that. Before she went to bed, she took her Bible and asked her mother to write out a list of verses to learn. She was surprised to find how easy it was to learn them. She learned one that night and another one every day. But the most surprising thing was how quickly the verses went to work.

Next morning on the way to Bible school, a dog started barking at Elaine. Usually she was afraid of dogs that barked at her, and she began to be afraid of this one. Then all of a sudden the verse she learned the night before jumped into her mind and said, "I will trust and not be afraid." And sure enough, she wasn't nearly as frightened as she usually was, and soon the dog went away.

On the way to school a few weeks later, a girl started to say some mean things about another child in their room. Usually Elaine was glad to listen, and sometimes she said mean things too. But this morning another of those verses jumped into her mind and said, "Let no corrupt communication proceed out of your mouth." Elaine's mother had told her this meant that we shouldn't say mean things. So she said quickly, "Let's run to school and see if we can get there early today." Then Elaine started talking about something else, and the other girl forgot the other things she was going to say.

That night Elaine's mother wanted her to wash the dishes. Elaine was just ready to say, "Oh, Mother, I can't do them tonight. I'm too tired." But just as she was going to say it, another of those Bible verses popped into her mind. This one said, "Children, obey your parents in the Lord for this is right." So Elaine closed her mouth and went out and started doing the dishes.

The next week Elaine wrote Elizabeth a letter and she said,

> I'm glad you told me about the camp you could go to because you learned five hundred verses. I am learning verses now, too. The verses I am learning are fine friends. They keep telling me the things I should do. I am glad I can learn the verses even though I can't go to camp.
>
> Your cousin,
> ELAINE

Questions:

1. Why was Elaine glad, even though she couldn't go to camp?
2. How many Bible verses do you know?
3. Are the verses you know good friends? Do you let them help you?

A Scripture verse:

I have thought much about Your words, and stored them in my heart so that they would hold me back from sin *(Psalm 119:11).*

A hymn to sing:

> Sing them over again to me,
> Wonderful words of Life;
> Let me more of their beauty see,
> Wonderful words of Life.

42

Ming Po Goes to School

This story happened several years ago in China. Ming Po lived in a town in China where there were many soldiers. There were soldiers at almost every street corner, and Ming Po didn't like to go to school because sometimes they laughed at him or teased him. Another reason Ming Po didn't like to go to school was because the teacher told the children that it was silly to believe in God and in Jesus. Ming Po knew that this was not true. He loved Jesus just as his father and mother did. He knew many Bible verses and used to go to Sunday school every Sunday morning until the soldiers came. After that there wasn't any Sunday school because teachers weren't allowed to be there. The soldiers told the teachers to go home and not to teach the children about Jesus.

One day when Ming Po was in school the teacher asked the children how many of them used to go to Sunday school. Many put up their hands. Then the teacher asked how many still went. None of them put up their hands. "That is good," said the teacher. "It is not good to go to Sunday school, because there they teach you about Jesus. Sunday school is a bad place."

"But, teacher," said Ming Po, "I think Sunday school is a very good place because it teaches us to love Jesus, and Jesus is our Savior. He died for our sins."

The room became very quiet, and the children were frightened because of what Ming Po had said. They knew that the teacher didn't want to hear about Jesus.

The teacher said, "Ming Po, do you love Jesus?"

"Yes," said Ming Po.

"Then," said the teacher, "you can stand in that corner, Ming Po, until you learn better!" It was about nine thirty in the morning when Ming Po had to go and stand in the corner. He had to stay there all the rest of the morning. He couldn't go home for lunch but had to stay in the corner all during the lunchtime and all afternoon, even during recess. He got very, very tired standing there, but the teacher would not let him sit down.

When the teacher finally let him go home, Ming Po went home to tell his mother and father what had happened. They already knew because some of the other children had told them.

"Ming Po," said his father, "some day the soldiers may come and take me away and shoot me because I love the Lord Jesus. We must be strong and brave and trust God. I am very proud of you for what you have done today. You have proved that you really love the Lord Jesus, and Jesus was watching from heaven. Jesus is very happy. No matter what they do to you, remember that Jesus loves you."

Since then other things have happened to make Ming Po very sad, but he always remembers that Jesus loves him.

Children in America should pray for the Christian children in China. Will you pray for them?

Questions:

1. Did the soldiers want the children to go to Sunday school?
2. Was Ming Po afraid to say he loved Jesus?
3. Why did he have to stand in the corner? How long did he have to stay there?
4. Do you think you should pray for the children in China?

A Scripture verse:

When you are reviled and persecuted and lied about because you are my followers—wonderful! Be happy about it! Be very glad! for a tremendous reward awaits you up in heaven *(Matthew 5:11-12)*.

A hymn to sing:

The whole world was lost in the darkness of sin;
The Light of the world is Jesus;
Like sunshine at noonday His glory shone in,
The Light of the world is Jesus.

43

Grandfather's Story

"**G**randfather," said the children crowding around him, "will you tell us another story?"

"Yes," said Susan, "tell us a story, please, about when you were a little boy."

"Were you a good boy or a bad boy?" asked Jill.

"Well," Grandfather said, laughing, "I guess I can tell you a story. As to whether I was a good boy or a bad boy, I would say I was both. Sometimes I was very good, and sometimes I was very bad. I remember I was bad enough to have many spankings."

"Oh," said Charles, "that was too bad! Did you love Jesus when you were a boy, as you do now?"

"I love Jesus very much now," said Grandfather, "but when I was a little boy I don't believe that I loved Jesus at all."

"But, Grandfather," said Jill, "You told us once that you got a prize for learning three hundred Bible verses when you were a little boy."

"Sure," said Grandfather, "I did. But I didn't love Jesus. In fact, it was the week after I had won my prize for memorizing all those Bible verses that something happened at school that I think I had better tell you about."

And this is Grandfather's story:

"One of the other boys had brought some money to school because he was going to stop at the store on the way home and buy a birthday present for his little brother. I knew he had the money because he showed it to me and asked me what I thought he ought to buy with it. Do you know what I told him?"

"No," said Jill, "what did you tell him to get?"

"I told him not to get a birthday present for his little brother, but instead to use the money to buy two ice cream cones, one for him and one for me."

"Oh," said Jill, "that wasn't nice at all! Is that what he did with the money?"

"No," said Grandfather, "he was a boy who loved Jesus, and knew that Jesus wanted him to be kind to his little brother. So he wouldn't buy the ice cream cones.

"And then the worst thing of all happened. That morning, after recess, all the other boys had hung up their coats. I stayed in the coatroom and found the money in his coat and took it."

"Oh, Grandfather!" Jill cried. "Why did you do such a thing? Did the boy know you took it?"

"No," said Grandfather, "he never found out, and I never told him. I still remember how sad he looked as he was walking home from school. He thought he had lost the money somewhere."

"But, Grandfather," Jill asked, "how could you do that when you had just earned a prize for saying three hundred Bible verses?"

"Well," said Grandfather, "the trouble was that I wasn't a Christian. A boy can learn a lot of Bible verses, and he can talk a lot about Jesus, but that doesn't mean he is a Christian. I went to Sunday school every Sunday morning, but that didn't make me a Christian. In fact, I didn't become a Christian for years and years."

Jill thought and thought before she asked the next question. She said, "Grandfather, if you learned all those verses and went to Sunday school and still weren't a Christian, how can I know whether I am a Christian or not?"

"The best way to know," Grandfather said gently, "is to notice how you act. If you have accepted the Lord Jesus and are kind and good then the Bible tells us that we can know that we are Christians. But if we are always doing wrong things, then perhaps we are not Christians at all, even though we say and think we are."

"If we are good enough, then can we be Christians?" Jill wanted to know.

"No," said Grandfather. "We are Christians only when Jesus saves us. Then He helps us want to do right things."

"I'm glad you told us that story," Jill said. "Now we know that we are not Christians just because we say we are. We have to act like Christians too. That is the way we can prove that Jesus is in our hearts."

Questions:

1. How many verses did Grandfather know when he was a boy?
2. Was Grandfather a Christian because he knew the verses?
3. What is a Christian?

A Scripture verse:

You try to look like saintly men, but underneath those pious robes are hearts besmirched with every sort of hypocrisy and sin *(Matthew 23:28)*.

A hymn to sing:

What can wash away my sin?
Nothing but the blood of Jesus;
What can make me whole again?
Nothing but the blood of Jesus.

44

Baby Rabbits

"**H**ey, Bill, come see my new rabbit," called Ron to his friend.

Ron was pulling tender green grass and pushing it through the wire of his rabbit's cage. The rabbit was a big white fluffy-looking one with long ears and pink eyes.

"Where did you get it?" Bill asked. Bill loved rabbits, but his mother wouldn't let him have one.

"I bought her for a dollar from Butch. She's going to have some babies in a few days. Then I'll have probably seven or eight rabbits instead of one."

"Wow!" Bill was surprised. "How do you know?"

"You can tell because she's so fat."

Bill felt the rabbit's sides, and his eyes glowed. "Why, you can even feel the babies."

"Yes," said Ron proudly, "and they almost always have six or eight babies at a time. She's already building a nest there in the corner with straw from the floor. Just before the babies are born, she pulls fur out from that big ball of fur under her neck and puts it around the nest to keep the babies warm."

"Don't the babies have fur on them when they're born?" Bill wanted to know.

"No, just pink skin," explained Ron, "just like a real baby."

"Wow!" said Bill. "I wonder how the mother rabbits know how to do all that. I think God must help them to know lots of things. He sure takes care of rabbits."

"Yes," said Ron, "and I guess if He takes care of rabbits He'll take care of us."

The next day Bill ran over to Ron's place right after church, and sure enough, there was fur all over the nest. At first he didn't see anything inside, but pretty soon he heard some weak noises and saw fur moving. Ron put his hands into the fur and pulled out the funniest-looking baby rabbit. It really didn't look like a rabbit at all! It was pink and its eyes were closed, and it didn't have any fur.

It was a little bit cold outside. Bill said, "Put it back in the nest, Ron. That's where God wants it to be. I still wonder what would happen if God let a mother rabbit forget to build a nest."

"Don't worry about it," Ron said. "God doesn't let them forget."

Questions:

1. How does God take care of baby rabbits?
2. How does the mother rabbit know how to make a nest?
3. Can you think of some ways God takes care of you?

A Scripture verse:

He is always thinking about you and watching everything that concerns you *(1 Peter 5:7).*

A hymn to sing:

Jesus loves me! this I know,
For the Bible tells me so;
Little ones to Him belong;
They are weak, but He is strong.
Yes, Jesus loves me,
Yes, Jesus loves me,
Yes, Jesus loves me—
The Bible tells me so.

45

Nancy's Allowance

Nancy was unhappy. It seemed as though Nancy was always unhappy. But this afternoon she was even more unhappy than usual. She was in the candy store, and she didn't have enough money to buy the candy as she wanted. She had only ten cents left out of the fifteen-cent allowance her father had given her that morning, and she wanted to buy twenty cents' worth of candy. She felt very cross, especially at her father because he hadn't given her a bigger allowance.

Nancy watched to see what the other children were buying. She noticed that Marilyn Rogers bought a sucker and gave the store clerk a dime. It was all that Marilyn had, but she didn't seem to mind. In fact, she seemed happy.

That night when her father came home, Nancy said, "Daddy, I must have a bigger allowance. I need to buy more candy. I need to buy lots of things to have fun with. It makes me unhappy when I can't buy the things I want."

But Nancy's father didn't think that would be a good idea at all. "It's not that I don't have the money to give you, Nancy," he said, "but money doesn't make people happy. You can never get enough money. The more you have, the more you want. If I give you twenty-five cents instead of fifteen cents, then you will want fifty cents. If I give you fifty cents, then you will want a dollar —and you'll still be unhappy."

"No," said Nancy, "if you give me twenty-five cents instead of fifteen cents I'll be very happy."

Nancy's father finally agreed. Nancy jumped with joy. She threw her arms around her father and said, "I think you're the best daddy in the whole world."

Her father shook his head. "You won't think so very long," he said. "Not if it depends on how much money I give you."

Nancy was happy for two whole days. She kept thinking, "Now I am rich. I have a twenty-five-cent allowance instead of only fifteen cents. Now I can be happy."

But the third day when Nancy went down to the candy store, she found she had only five cents left because she had already spend twenty of the twenty-five cents her father had given her. *Oh, dear,* she thought, *only five cents left. I've simply got to have a larger allowance. My father is stingy. He ought to give me fifty cents.*

She told Marilyn what she thought, but Marilyn only smiled. "I get only ten cents for my allowance," she said, "but that doesn't make me unhappy."

"How can you be so happy, Marilyn, when you have only a ten-cent allowance?" Nancy asked.

"Oh, that's easy," said Marilyn. "I'm happy because I have so many things. I have a nice home, a dear mother and daddy, happy brothers and sisters, a good school to go to, and all kinds of nice things. But most of all I have Jesus. I could still be happy if I didn't have so many things that please me, if I just had Him. He makes me happy."

Nancy was very surprised. "Jesus must be a nice Friend," she said, "if He can make you happy even when you have only a small allowance. Maybe what I need is Jesus, instead of more money."

Marilyn thought so too. She told Nancy all about Jesus, and invited her to come to Sunday school with her so that Nancy could learn more.

And do you know what happened? Nancy became a friend of Jesus, and that isn't all. One day she told her father, "Daddy, I need only a fifteen-cent allowance now, just the same as I used to get."

Nancy's father, who was not a Christian, looked surprised. "How come?" he wanted to know.

"Because," Nancy explained, "money doesn't make you happy; only Jesus can do that."

"I guess you're right," her father said. "Maybe I'd better find out about Jesus too."

Questions:

1. Did the larger allowance make Nancy happy? What did she want then?
2. Do you have enough money? Will you ever have enough?
3. How can Jesus make us happy?

A Scripture verse:

Be content with such things as you have *(1 Timothy 6:10)*.

A hymn to sing:

> Count your blessings
> Name them one by one;
> Count your blessings,
> See what God hath done;
> Count your blessings,
> Name them one by one;
> Count your many blessings,
> See what God hath done.

46

The Fourth of July Worm

Tomorrow would be the Fourth of July. There would be a parade in the afternoon, and at night there would be fireworks with rockets and Roman candles and firecrackers and bombs down in the park where everyone could see them.

But there was something even more interesting than that for Roy and his friends. The candy lady at the store across from school was selling little boxes of what looked like aspirin tablets, but they weren't. Instead they were a very special kind of tablet. If you lit them with a match, they would begin to burn very slowly and start to wiggle. Out of the burning would come a long, twisty worm about six inches long. When the tablet had finished burning, there wouldn't be any tablet at all. There would be just the worm. Of course it wasn't a real worm, and after the tablet had disappeared, it would just lie there cold and dead. But it was great fun to watch it coming out of the burning tablet.

All of the children in the neighborhood had bought boxes of these tablets except Roy. He didn't have any money, and tomorrow was the Fourth of July. There was only one box left when Roy went into the store to see, so he was very sad.

While Roy was looking at the box of tablets, a big girl named Donna who lived near Roy, came in. She saw that he wanted the box of tablets very badly. When Roy told her that he didn't have any money to buy the box, she said to the candy lady, "Here is twenty-five cents. I would like that box to give to Roy." And so Roy got his box of tablets!

Roy was a happy as a lark. He ran out of the store and ran home to get a box of matches from his mother. She helped him light one of the tablets. Sure enough the longest, nicest, most wriggly worm you have ever seen came out of the tablet. But then do you know what happened?

Mother went into the house, and Donna came along and said, "Roy, would you come to my house and show some people your box of worms?" Roy was glad to do this, but when he got to Donna's house, she said, "This is my box of worms that I gave to Roy. Wasn't that nice of me?" That made Roy feel very unhappy and disappointed. Roy didn't think that the box of tablets was really a nice gift from Donna. He felt that Donna had not been fair in giving him the box if she just wanted to show off about what a nice girl she was when she bought it for him.

And Roy was right. The Lord Jesus tells us not to show off about the good things we do. If we are kind because we love Him, then we ought not to tell anybody else about how nice we are. We should be kind so we may please Jesus, not to make our friends think that we are nice people.

Questions:

1. Did Donna give the box of tablets to Roy because she was kind? Why did she do it?
2. Should we tell people how kind and good we are?

A Scripture verse:

Take care! Don't do your good deeds publicly, to be admired *(Matthew 6:1)*.

A hymn to sing:

> True-hearted, whole-hearted, faithful and loyal,
> King of our lives, by Thy grace we will be;
> Under the standard exalted and royal,
> Strong in Thy strength we will battle for Thee.

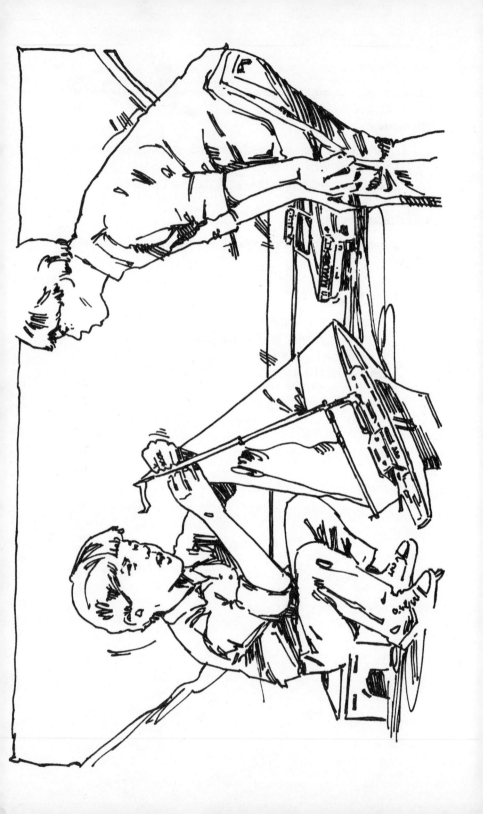

47

The Quarrelsome Boy

It seemed to Mother that she had never heard so much quarreling! Perhaps it was because it was a rainy Saturday and John and Greg couldn't go outside to play. First the boys quarreled about washing and drying the dishes. Then they quarreled about who was going to play with the big truck and who was going to have the little truck. Then they quarreled about playing at the same place on the floor at the same time.

Finally Mother couldn't stand it any longer. "If you boys don't stop quarreling," she said, "both of you are going to have to go up to your beds and stay there the rest of the morning." When Mother said that, there was a sudden silence, and the boys quit pushing and growling at each other.

"OK," said John, "you can play here if you want to. I'm going over to that corner there."

"Oh, no," said Greg, "I'm going over there. You stay here."

All of a sudden both boys started laughing. "It sure is funny," Greg said. "We were quarreling because we both wanted to be in the same spot on the floor, and now we are quarreling because neither of us wants to be there."

John said, "I guess it really wasn't that we wanted to be in the same spot. It was just that we felt quarrelsome and had to have something to fight about."

"I think you're right," said Mother. "If there is a quarrel in your heart, it will come out, and you will start a quarrel with anyone about anything."

"I would sure like to get Mr. Quarrel out of my heart," said Greg, "so he wouldn't always be starting trouble."

"I think we can," John said. "If we ask Jesus, He will make Mr. Quarrel stay away, and Mr. Happy will come into our hearts instead."

"But that wouldn't work very well," Greg said. "If you didn't quarrel about things, then people would always have their own way. You'd never get things you ought to have. Somebody else would always have his way, and you would never have yours."

Then Mother said, "But that is the Christian way. Most things we quarrel about are not very important, and Mr. Happy doesn't worry about whether he gets to play with something first or not. Since Jesus loves him, he wants to be loving and kind to other people even when they are unkind."

Then John had another thought. "But if each of us is letting the other do things first, then neither of us will get to do them, because we will each be waiting for the other person to do it first."

Mother laughed. "I wouldn't worry about that," she said. "I think you can decide whose turn it is."

"Yes," said Greg, "we wouldn't want to quarrel about whose turn it was to be nice."

Then Mother and both boys laughed and laughed—to think about quarreling over being nice!

And for some reason the rest of the morning was happy even if it was rainy outside. Mr. Quarrel must have gone outside into the rain, because he wasn't in the house at all.

Questions:

1. What were the boys quarreling about?
2. If we feel quarrelsome inside, can we always find things to quarrel about?
3. If we feel happy and kind inside, can we find things to quarrel about?
4. How can we be happy and kind?

A Scripture verse:

They must not speak evil of anyone, nor quarrel, but be gentle and truly courteous to all *(Titus 3:2)*.

A hymn to sing:

> O there's sunshine, blessed sunshine,
> When the peaceful, happy moments roll;
> When Jesus shows His smiling face,
> There is sunshine in my soul.

48

Saved on a Raft

Ken and his family were having a vacation. They were living in
a little cabin on a big island. There was some shallow water for
Ken to play in. He couldn't swim very well, so his mother had told
him to be careful not to go out too far. Ken had a raft to play on
and a pole so that he could push the raft along near the shore.

One afternoon when Ken was pushing the raft he noticed a
funny bug sitting on one of the boards of the raft, and he looked at
it for a long time. When he finally started to pick up his pole to
push the raft farther, he was surprised and scared to see that the
raft was a long way from shore. While Ken was looking at the
bug, the raft had been moving away from the land, and it was still
moving!

Ken called loudly for help. Finally his mother, who was in the
cabin, heard him. She came running down to the water.

"Kenneth! Kenneth!" she called. "Come back at once."

"But I can't," Ken shouted. "I don't know how I got here,
and I can't get back. The pole won't reach the bottom."

Ken's mother ran down to the water and jumped in. She
swam and swam. Finally she reached the raft. She was very tired
when she got there. After she had rested a few minutes she began to swim toward shore, pulling the raft slowly along with her.

It was hard work. It was a long time before the raft came to shore.

That night when Ken was being tucked into bed his mother said, "Ken, what happened this afternoon can remind us about how Jesus saves us. You were going farther and farther away from home, and you couldn't do anything to get back. You wer. helpless. Then you called for help, and Mother heard you and was willing to risk her life to save you.

"This is the way it is with our heavenly home. We had sinned against God and were getting farther and farther away from Him. Then God sent Jesus to save us. Jesus died for us. He died for the punishment of our sins and will bring us home to heaven where we can live forever. Mother saved you this morning for a little while, but Jesus can save you forever."

After Mother had kissed him good night, Ken got out of bed and knelt beside his bed and talked to God. "Thank You for letting Mother save me this morning," he said. "And I want Jesus to be my Savior forever. Thank You for dying for my sins."

Questions:

1. Why didn't Ken notice that he was getting farther away from the shore?
2. What did he do when he found out?
3. What should we do when we see that we have sinned?
4. Can we save ourselves?

A Scripture verse:

And the real life I now have within this body is a result of my trusting in the Son of God, who loved me and gave Himself for me *(Galatians 2:20)*.

A hymn to sing:

We have heard the joyful sound:
Jesus saves! Jesus saves!
Spread the tidings all around:
Jesus saves! Jesus saves!